Belchertown

Belchertown

Bits of History

Collected Writings of Doris and Harvey Dickinson

EDITED BY CLIFF MCCARTHY AND DORIS DICKINSON

Charleston ⌐ London

History
PRESS

Published by The History Press
Charleston, SC 29403
www.historypress.net

Cover image: A postcard view of the Methodist church on Belchertown Common.

First published 2007

Manufactured in the United Kingdom

ISBN 978.1.59629.264.2

Library of Congress Cataloging-in-Publication Data

Belchertown : bits of history / edited by Cliff McCarthy and Doris Dickinson.
    p. cm.
  ISBN 978-1-59629-264-2 (alk. paper)
1. Belchertown (Mass. : Town)--History--Anecdotes. 2. Belchertown (Mass. : Town)--Social life and customs--Anecdotes. 3. Belchertown (Mass. : Town)--Biography--Anecdotes. I. McCarthy, Cliff. II. Dickinson, Doris M.
  F74.B207B45 2007
  974.4'23--dc22
                                    2007005208

Pages 12 and 13: A pick-up baseball game at the south end of the Common, circa early 1900s.

Pages 40 and 41: The pavilion at Dyer's Pond, which once gave respite from the summer heat to guests of the Park View Hotel.

Pages 72 and 73: The Belchertown Fair is the highlight of the autumn season. This postcard view shows the crowd on the Common for the Belchertown Cattle Show, as it was known in the early 1900s.

Pages 102 and 103: A winter scene from the south end of the Common.

Contents

Harvey Dickinson
1923–2006

From the top of his funny hats to the tip of his "geezer shoes," Harvey Dickinson loved people. He had a knack for making people—all kinds of people—feel comfortable and at ease. Unlike the politician whose glad-handing leaves you checking your wallet, Harvey's motives were pure. He was charitable with both his time and money. He simply hated to see people in distress.

The Belchertown Historical Association was one of the beneficiaries of Harvey's volunteerism. He gave countless hours to helping us continue our mission of preserving the history of the area. Typically, he worked behind the scenes: fixing things that needed fixing, setting up and taking down tables and chairs for events and adding his memories to our body of knowledge of the Swift River Valley. He wrote some of those reminiscences for publication in the *Belchertown Sentinel* and for the senior center newsletter. He was also an active member, board member and tour guide for the Swift River Historical Society in New Salem.

Harvey was born in Greenwich, Massachusetts, in 1923, the son of storekeeper and postmaster Howard H. Dickinson and his wife, the former Ruby Thresher. The Dickinsons moved to Belchertown when Greenwich was flooded for the creation of the Quabbin Reservoir, establishing the family home in the Thomson house on South Main Street. Harvey served his country during World War II by enlisting in the U.S. Navy, where he was stationed in—of all places—Oklahoma. It was there that he met his wife and lifelong partner, Doris, and when he brought her to Belchertown to live after the war, our community benefited in innumerable ways. He was a member of the Belchertown Congregational Church for more than fifty years and was also a member of the Mount Vernon Lodge of Masons. He enjoyed traveling throughout the United States and always came back with a good story or two. It is Belchertown's good fortune that they chose to live their sixty-two years together, and raise their five daughters, in our town.

On the topic of good fortune, one of my favorite pieces that Harvey wrote for the *Sentinel* is entitled "Luck" and is included in this book. It recounts how dying baseball player Lou Gehrig considered himself "the luckiest man on the face of the earth." It reminds us of how luck is relative to one's station in the world and that we all, here in this place, have much to be thankful for. Harvey wrote, "For those persons whose misfortunes are more than can be coped with, it is for us, the lucky ones, to share some of our good fortune…So as this new year approaches, let us give thanks for our good luck and in the New Year resolve to pay more heed to the needs of our less lucky fellow beings." This, Harvey Dickinson did, every day, in the way he lived his life.

Cliff McCarthy

Opposite: Harvey and Doris Dickinson vacationing at Prince Edward Island in the late 1970s.

Introduction

This book contains bits of history. Belchertown's past is woven throughout each of the vignettes, which combine personal reminiscences with researched history to create a patchwork tapestry of this small but growing New England town. Within these fifty-two stories—one for each week of the year—the reader can feel the rhythm of the seasons and mark the passage of time through the changes it brings.

The stories that follow originally appeared in the *Belchertown Sentinel*, the local weekly newspaper that since 1915 has reported those changes and other town activities to the citizenry. Longtime Belchertown residents Doris and Harvey Dickinson have delighted the newspaper's readers over the years with their memories, their insights, experiences and considerable knowledge of the town's past. Doris's column in that paper is called Bits of History. This book would not be possible without the *Sentinel* and the cooperation of its current publishers, Turley Publications.

For many years, Bob Jackson wrote a column for the *Sentinel*—first called Soliloquies of a Steeple and later, The Steeple Soliloquizes—which chronicled the noteworthy events in town. As one source of good information, these columns are frequently mentioned in this book and are referred to collectively as his Steeple columns.

As archivist at the Stone House Museum, Doris Dickinson is at the perfect juncture of past and present. She is cataloguing, organizing and preserving the thousands of documents that tell the stories of the town, while interpreting and reporting on them to today's audiences. The Stone House Museum is the headquarters of the Belchertown Historical Association, to which the Dickinsons have devoted immeasurable amounts of their volunteer time and energy. The association has graciously allowed the use of many of the images that are included here. Proceeds from this endeavor will benefit the Belchertown Historical Association.

Spring

Spring Has Sprung—Almost

On March 17, St. Patrick's Day, the first robin appeared on my brown and dreary lawn. I had just hung out a small batch of laundry to dry for the first time, probably since this same robin left for the Southern climes last fall. Man and bird were of the same mind. Spring must be on its way.

The following day I observed several flocks of robins around town. We should not get carried away, at this point, and start planting our peas, for I am sure that nature will have its way with us yet. There can be some miserable weather in late March, and April can be a cruel month.

Another sign of spring, other than the arrival of the robins, is the Home Show at the Expo in West Springfield. I have always tried to avoid going, mostly because I hate to have to pay five dollars for the privilege of having someone try to sell me a vacuum cleaner or vinyl siding for my house. This year, senior citizens were able to attend free on March 17, and so, with my wife and a couple of friends, I gave it a try. To our surprise, it was nothing like we had imagined. It seemed that everything in the world that money could buy was there—and maybe even happiness, if that is owning a whirlpool bathtub as big as your living room. A visit to the Home Show is a good spring tonic.

My wife and daughter and I have recently returned from a short visit to the San Diego area where my wife's elderly aunt lives. We go to visit her at least once a year. We had several reasons to take the trip, but not the least of them was to escape—if only for a short time—the cold and gray days of late winter. This may be a rather expensive elixir, but stepping out of the airport into a warm sixty-five-degree evening has to raise one's spirits.

A San Diego winter is similar to some of our best May days in New England, with nights in the fifties and days in the seventies. Flowers and fruit trees are in full bloom. The surrounding hills and roadsides are a sea of ice plants and poppies. This is the only time of year that the grasses and shrubs on the hillsides are green and lush. When the New England winter starts to wear on you and you can't wait for spring, a visit to San Diego may be just the ticket.

You probably have noticed that I haven't mentioned the annual flight of the "Snowbirds." These are our friends who leave for Florida after Thanksgiving and come back around Easter, all tanned and healthy looking, with a bag of oranges as a peace offering. Those of us who are not retired or cannot afford it must stay here and put up with cold and slush and whatever else Mother Nature throws at us.

This winter has not been hard to take. At least we have not had to put up with much snow at all. On the other hand, sometimes the lack of a good snow cover adds to the boredom of a New England winter. At least snow would have hidden some of the leaves we never got around to raking last fall.

If you haven't seen your first robin, keep an eye out, for that may be the best spring tonic of all!

Harvey Dickinson

THE PARK ASSOCIATION

Patriots' Day has come and gone. It is a quintessential New England observance that commemorates an event in April 1775, more than two centuries ago. It marks the beginning of the American Revolutionary War, the skirmishes between the minutemen and the British troops in Concord and Lexington, preceded by Paul Revere's famous ride. Originally celebrated on April 19, Patriots' Day was moved to the third Monday of April in 1969. For modern day runners, Patriots' Day has become synonymous with the Boston Marathon.

April 19 in Belchertown used to be observed in a very special fashion. It was the day the Park Association designated as "Rake the Common" day. Just when that date was chosen for this spring ritual is not clear, but articles began to appear in the *Sentinel* in the 1920s and '30s urging a good turnout for the day. Just like those early residents who answered the call to march to Lexington, this time residents were called to the Common armed with rakes.

One article was headlined "To Rake the Common—Fair Weather or Foul." It went on to say, "Of course, as everyone knows, or ought to, this is the day to rake the Common, when everybody is invited to take a hand. No amount of flag waving today, Memorial Day or the Fourth of July will compensate for a little honest-to-goodness public spirit exercised today." Sometimes the Union Grange would serve a lunch. In later years, a picture of the hardy souls and the work accomplished would appear in the *Sentinel* to memorialize another successful day.

One of the first efforts made to beautify the Common came as a result of a sermon given in the Congregational church. On April 2, 1860, Reverend Dr. Samuel Wolcott preached a sermon on the "Cedars of Lebanon," urging the improvement of the Common. The next morning, he was on the Common with shovel in hand and he was not disappointed. He was joined by a large force of men. Trees were brought in from the surrounding woods and planted along the east side and along South Main Street.

It was during the nineteenth century that the greatest changes occurred on the commons of New England. Many reform movements were sweeping the country and one such movement proclaimed the advantages of open space and outdoor recreation. Two proponents were Calvert Vaux and Frederick Law Olmsted, whose names are synonymous with nineteenth century parks.

The village improvement movement started in 1853 in Stockbridge, Massachusetts, and many societies began forming, with members taking it upon themselves to clean up and beautify their respective villages. Belchertown became caught up in this movement. In response to a call signed by numerous citizens, on September 8, 1873, a public meeting was held to consider the subject of village improvement. It was decided to form a Park Association, and its constitution called for "the improvement of the public grounds, the cultivation of taste, and the promotion of a better acquaintance among the people of the Town." Soon after the first organizational meeting, it was determined to undertake the improvement of the Common.

At that time, the Common was crossed by wagons and carriages from the Post Office Corner (Masonic Hall) to the Congregational church and from the brick store (the building next to the Methodist Church) to the Congregational church and adjoining sheds. Many paths zigzagged across from corner to corner. Everett Clapp, of Belchertown and New York (a brother of Francis Clapp who left money for the Clapp Memorial Library), was very interested in the project and submitted a plan for the Common that included a fence to discourage teams from crossing it.

Clean-up day on the Common.

Spring

Preliminary to this undertaking, it was necessary to obtain the consent of the town. A town meeting was convened on September 29, 1873, at which four resolutions were passed without opposition. The first gave the association permission at its own expense to enclose the Common with a fence, set out shade and ornamental trees and otherwise improve and beautify the Common. The second gave the association, in concurrence with the selectmen, control over the Common so far as may be necessary to protect it from "unlawful depredations and mutilations." The third made it obligatory upon the selectmen, whenever the Park Association requested in writing, to appoint a policeman with authority to enforce the laws relating to public grounds and prosecute all offenders. The policeman was to be paid by the association. The fourth provided that the association could cut the grass upon the Common "at its pleasure, and appropriate for its own use, the income."

Everett Clapp and his brothers provided the money for the chain fence. It is said that the chain was of a "peculiar pattern" and imported from England at an expense of $500.

Winter weather set in early that year and little was accomplished, but the ladies of the organization were raising funds. A tea party netted ninety-one dollars. Mrs. Rebecca Dearborn organized and directed a series of dramatic readings, which realized forty dollars.

Spring saw work started again with a few hired men and some volunteers, but soon the treasury was in need of funds. The ladies came through and held a strawberry supper and raised $130 for the treasury. J.M. Towne was appointed superintendent of the project and "prosecuted it vigorously and successfully" until about the first of September, when all was ready for the fence to be erected. It was decided to have a grand rally on Monday, September 7, and set the posts in a single day, if possible. Announcement of the rally was read from all the pulpits. More than one hundred men responded and before twelve o'clock, 325 postholes were dug and a good beginning made before the more difficult work of setting the posts in line. The ladies provided a bountiful dinner in the town hall. About four o'clock, the hard work of the day being done, and the park with walks, and lawns and trees, being enclosed with a neat post and chain fence, people gathered around the Liberty Pole, where for the space of an hour songs were sung and speeches made. One was made by Everett Clapp, who received a rousing vote of thanks. A total of $1,587 was expended the first year of operation; the money being derived from donations, fundraisers, cash subscriptions and volunteer labor.

Over the years, they continued to maintain the "Park," as it was also called, as much as their limited funds would allow. The fence, which was erected on that day in September, fell into disrepair and was removed in 1904. Two of the wooden fence posts are now at the Stone House.

So, in later years the date of April 19 was designated Common Cleanup Day by the Park Association, and townspeople turned out to rake. The high school and seventh and eighth grades usually raked the day before, with rakes being donated by and left with Harold Peck at the A.H. Phillips Store. The last Common Cleanup Day was held on April 19, 1947. On May 17 of that year, the Park Association voted to 'waive all rights, privileges and responsibilities in regard to the tract of land known as the Common, which the town delegated to the Association Sept. 29, 1873" and to disband after almost seventy-five years of volunteer service to the town. This group had the unpaid privilege of cleaning the Common each spring, of planning for its improvement, of trying to arrange for its mowing, but had little control over its use or misuse.

Today, when we admire our Common, we need to remember and give thanks to the many members of the Park Association who helped to maintain its natural scenic beauty.

Doris Dickinson

CHARLES AND SARA ROBINSON

T he mail brings interesting letters to the Stone House. Last week, a little bit of Belchertown history arrived in a letter from the Kansas State Historical Society. It was an envelope addressed to Mrs. Sara T.D. Robinson in Lawrence, Kansas. The return address on the envelope was the "D.L. Hazen Department Store, Belchertown, Mass." Alas, there was nothing in the envelope. The envelope, with a two-cent stamp, left Belchertown on April 23, 1908 at 6:00 p.m. and arrived in Lawrence, Kansas, on April 25 at 11:00 p.m. I wonder if the U.S. mail could do as well today.

The Kansas State Historical Society had removed this envelope from their manuscript division's collection and thought it might be more appropriate for our collection. How right they were. Both names carry a lot of history. Sara Tappan Doolittle Lawrence was the daughter of Myron Lawrence, a Belchertown lawyer who was also president of the Massachusetts Senate for two years. D.L. Hazen was the owner of Hazen's Store in Belchertown. His wife, Clara Dwight Hazen, was one of Belchertown's early historians. There are some handwritten dates computed on the back of the envelope: 1908 minus 1894 equals fourteen and 1894 minus 1818 equals seventy-six. Had Clara D. Hazen, a distant cousin of Sara, asked for some bit of history? We are only left to guess the contents of the envelope.

Above left: Sara T.D. Lawrence Robinson as a young woman.

Above right: Sara T.D. Lawrence Robinson.

Sara Lawrence married Dr. Charles Robinson in 1851 and went to the Kansas territory with him in 1855. Dr. Robinson had become involved with the Immigrant Aid Company started by Amos Lawrence of Massachusetts (no relation to Sara), which was enlisting Massachusetts residents to take up land in the Kansas territory. This was during the time that the antislavery movement was gaining impetus in the North before the beginning of the Civil War. The settlers were of that persuasion and were determined to make Kansas a "Free State." They established the town of Lawrence, Kansas—named for Amos Lawrence of Massachusetts—and christened its two streets "Massachusetts" and "Vermont." Dr. Robinson went on to become the first territorial governor of Kansas and its first governor under statehood.

Sara Robinson was a resident of Kansas for fifty-three years, but she never forgot her New England home. Upon her death, she left the residue of her estate to build a hall in Belchertown to honor her father and mother. Most residents know it as the town hall, but to be correct, when you go to pay your taxes, you are entering Lawrence Memorial Hall.

Mrs. Robinson had purchased the property where the old Highland Hotel had stood. The hotel had burned in the late 1800s and the land had remained vacant. When the hall was to be erected in the early 1920s, another event occurred. The high school—which was located where Center School now stands—burned, leaving the town without a high school. The selectmen, being shrewd Yankees, went to probate court to see if they could incorporate a high school into the hall. This was granted and that is how the town got not only a hall for town use, but also a new high school, which was built at the rear of the building.

The front entrance is no longer used as the main entrance, but if you enter the hall from that entrance you will find portraits of Governor Robinson and Sara Robinson; her father, the Honorable Myron Lawrence; her sister, Mrs. Sophia Dwight Goddard; and her nephew, Frank D. Lawrence. The portrait of her mother, Clarissa Dwight Lawrence, hangs over the Hepplewhite sideboard in the Stone House Museum. It seems unfortunate that the hall, which held many town functions including town meetings, graduations, minstrel shows, class plays and dances, now seems to be the repository of excess furniture and temporary meeting rooms. I wonder what Sara thinks of this as she looks down from the wall.

Doris Dickinson

PUMP LOGS

As I drove along Route 9 this week and saw all the excavation and the piles of pipe for the sewer lines, it brought to mind an unusual artifact at the Stone House Museum that has reposed almost hidden in the Ford Annex for over fifty years. In the spring of 1950, Bob Hanifin was plowing on his farm near Cold Spring and he uncovered an artifact. Subsequently, a small article appeared in the *Belchertown Sentinel* with the headline "Ancient Wooden Pipe." The article went on to say, "An acquisition this past week at the Stone House is a piece of wooden pipe that Bob Hanifin plowed up near the Cold Spring, located on his farm, and for which the town was originally named. Mr. Hanifin thinks this may have been part of a pipe line that possibly went to the Moriarty place, the site of a tavern in the old stage coach days. The piece of pipe looks like an old fence post hollowed out through the center." After doing some research, I found that this small piece of history was called a pump log.

If there is one thing about the Yankee farmer, it is his ability to make do with what is available. I have not been able to discover where or when the first pump logs were used. Some pioneer with an inventive frame of mind must have conceived the idea of wooden pipes to convey water by gravity from a spring to the farm buildings. For that reason, I don't think the pipe that Bob Hanifin plowed up in his field was to the Moriarty home (demolished just over a year ago) since the house was uphill from the site. But there is a hill behind where that house stood and there could have been a water system using pump logs from the springs behind the house. A tavern would have needed a great deal of water.

In New England there was plenty of wood, especially the small diameter, straight white pine, spruce or poplar, easily worked and long-lasting when in constant contact with moist soil. Pipes were made by boring a hole, an inch to an inch-and-a-half in diameter, for the length of an eight-foot log. The end of one log was tapered by using a sheep's head auger. This device could be likened to a pencil sharpener. Another log was reamed at one end so that when the two logs were placed—tapered end to reamed end—they would fit together. When the wood became wet in the ground the logs would swell and fit tightly together making a leak-proof pipe. The Shelburne Museum in Shelburne, Vermont, has a whole set of pump log tools.

It must have been a wonderful day on a farm when a housewife could dip water from a barrel beside the kitchen sink instead of carrying it by bucket from a spring, brook or well. Farmers could let their livestock out to drink at a trough in the barnyard. The heyday of pump log use was from about 1750 to 1850. In the 1850s, machinery evolved to bore the logs with treadmill horsepower.

Who knows how long this piece of history lay hidden till brought to the light of day during spring plowing? Was that "never failing" spring the source of some early water supply? Who bored the holes and installed the pipes on this rocky hillside that now provides a bountiful supply of fruit? We will probably never know, but sometimes when I see an excavation for a new building or house, a trench being dug or a bulldozer at work, I stop and see if another bit of history has surfaced.

Doris Dickinson

McKinney's Tavern

Nothing but a cellar hole with blackened timbers and an ell with the remnants of a beehive oven are left of what was one of Belchertown's oldest homes. In the spring of this year, the Belchertown Fire Department, at the request of the property owners, burned the house in a practice session, leaving these stark remains.

Located on Cold Spring Road, the house was once a tavern on the old road between Northampton and Boston. Located about a quarter of a mile from the famous spring that gave the town its first name, Cold Spring Plantation, it had long stood with broad fields surrounding the house and a panoramic view of the Holyoke range. L.H. Everts, in his *History of the Connecticut Valley*, says that Samuel Shaw erected a public house near Cold Spring at an early date, and it was first kept by a man named McKinney. Deeds show that Shaw purchased the property in 1819 and sold it to Charles McKinney in 1822.

Once McKinney's Tavern, this building was known as the Moriarty house in the 1980s.

In *Along the County Road*, published in 1982 by the Belchertown Historical Commission, the house is described as follows: "The front portion, a large two-story center hall farmhouse, was built as a tavern, circa 1819. The low back el, with its steeply pitched roof, was possibly the home of Isaac Livermore built on this site, circa 1778." Isaac Livermore served in the Revolution and participated in Daniel Shays' Rebellion, later moving to New York state. He is listed in the first census in 1790 as living in Belchertown with two males under sixteen years of age and five females.

From 1835 to 1866, the property was owned by Samuel Austin Shaw. Morris Moriarty purchased the property in 1874 and several generations of that family farmed these acres of land that extended west all the way to Franklin Street. About the same time, in 1877, John Flaherty purchased land down the road from Morris Moriarty. *Along the County Road* states, "The Flaherty, Moriarty, Sullivan, Garvey and Austin families were among the first Irish Catholic families to settle in Belchertown. These families settled here in the 1850s on farms in South Belchertown as the native sons were leaving for the industrialized cities and the golden west."

The spring is still there on land now owned by the University of Massachusetts. Remnants of the old road, which felt the rumbling stagecoaches on their way to Boston, can still be traveled, but no tavern is there to give respite to the weary traveler. What will be the next chapter for this land that has seen so much of Belchertown history?

Doris Dickinson

GRITS

You know that you are in the South when a waitress asks, "Y'all want greyettes with your breakfast?" The word "grits" is often pronounced that way below the Mason-Dixon Line. In the North, you are often asked if you want home fries. Another way of knowing you are in the South is seeing a dead armadillo aside the road. Some people place grits and these dead critters in the same category. Another sign of the South is the Palmetto, a squatty plant somewhat like our Yucca. The Snowbirds that drive south for the winter must be happy when they first see these signs that warmth is not far away.

On a fishing trip to Florida, my companion, Charlie, looked at the heap of grits piled up on my breakfast plate and asked if I was really going to eat that stuff. Of course, I said, when in Rome, I do as the Romans do. We were about a hundred miles from Rome, Georgia, at the time, but Charlie's hangover interfered with his global positioning. Charlie had never strayed far from the Connecticut Valley, so my little fib was not questioned.

I like grits. They are easy to prepare. If you can boil water, you can have grits. As a breakfast dish, they look and taste like Cream of Wheat, which is actually farina. They test best if you add butter, milk, cream, sugar or best of all, maple syrup. This is "stick to your ribs" kind of stuff. Grits can be used as a side dish when you add salt, pepper and butter or gravy. Another way to enjoy grits is by frying them. Pour a batch onto a flat pan or cookie sheet while still warm, making a layer about a half-inch thick. Brown in a pan with butter and serve sweetened with maple syrup.

Grits are made from corn. The kernels are treated by a process called "mixtamalization" (yes, I had to look it up), which is a fancy word for removal of the hulls by soaking in lye or lime. The product is known as hulled corn or hominy. After drying, the hulled kernels are ground to make grits. The process has been used by Central Americans for ten thousand years.

I am a cereal lover as you may suspect—cornmeal mush, rolled oats, rolled wheat, Wheaties, Corn Flakes, Shredded Wheat, etc. I had to throw away part of a box of Count Chocula left over from the grandchildren's visit. To me, chocolate flavored cereal has about the same appeal as garlic flavored ice cream.

As a kid, I don't remember sitting down often to breakfast as a family. We all had different starting times. My time was the last, just minutes before leaving for school. I didn't have time for what was called a good breakfast—bacon, eggs and toast.

For the first twenty-five years of my life, we had a cow. This meant thick, spoonable cream, whole milk, butter and cottage cheese. I bring this up because it leads to another cereal favorite: Shredded Wheat biscuits wetted with very hot water and butter melted on top, the milk, cream and sugar added. I blame our cow for my heart attack fifty years later. Cholesterol dangers, at that time of my childhood, had not been explored.

I have digressed from my grits topic, and I wonder if there are any grits eaters among my readers. Am I alone in this thing?

Harvey Dickinson

DEVON LANE FARM

A barn on Daniel Shays Highway recently received a new roof. A new roof on a barn is not necessarily news, but this roof has an interesting design incorporated into the shingles. The design is a tractor.

The barn, which once housed Devon cattle, now is the home of Devon Lane Farm Supply. About forty years ago, when the barn needed a roof, a local carpenter named Julian Hussey took the liberty of designing the first tractor design for the roof. So this new roof carries on that tradition. I seem to recall that someone remarked years ago that the planes flying into Westover after practice bombing runs over the Quabbin Reservoir would use that roof as a marker. But that is not the end of the story.

Luther and Nellie Shattuck brought their family from Alberta, Canada, to live in Belchertown in 1931. They bought a farm on Pelham Road. This road passed between the Shattuck home and the barn. The building of the Quabbin Reservoir eliminated part of the road, so the state planned a new route. The new road would have passed only a few feet from the barn, so the state moved the barn. It now sits on the west side of Route 202, Daniel Shays' Highway.

Ira Shattuck once described the moving in this manner:

> *My father moved the barn in 1934. A tremendous project even for nowadays, it was quite a feat then. A steam-fired machine, with a hand-operated scoop dug out the foundation. The barn itself was moved on trestles. The workers did such a good job that the mud swallows never even moved and the barn was only a few inches off on one corner when it was set down on the new foundation.*

An accident in 1954 left Ira paralyzed from the neck down and in a wheelchair. Obviously, he could no longer run the farm that his parents had started. He had a wife and four small children to support. Prior to his accident, he had begun to sell a few pieces of farm machinery. That small beginning was the start of Devon Lane Farm Supply, which is still housed in that barn. His two sons, William and Thomas, later joined him in the business. Mr. Shattuck died May 5, 1998. William Shattuck

The Shattucks' barn at Devon Lane Farm on Daniel Shays Highway.

The Shattucks' farm before Daniel Shays Highway was built.

and his son are now managing Devon Lane Farm Supply and Thomas Shattuck and his sons have opened Devon Lane Power Equipment on Route 9. The fourth generation of the Shattuck family still lives on the farm, and Devon cattle, which were quite a novelty in 1931, still graze in the fields on Daniel Shays Highway.

Doris Dickinson

THE DAY BELCHERTOWN WAS BOMBED

"The Day Belchertown was Bombed" could have been the headline, but editor Lewis Blackmer was not into big headlines. A small article in the May 19, 1944 edition of the *Belchertown Sentinel* had the heading "Bomb Drops on North Main Street." The article read,

An unexploded, 100 pound practice bomb dropped last week near the Kempkes home on North Main Street, in the lot back of the house, the spot being possibly 300 feet from the building. Even though the bomb did not explode, it buried itself in the earth about four feet and made a crater of about that distance across. Men from Westover came Wednesday and extracted the missile.

Intrigued by the article, I contacted Joseph Kempkes Jr. to learn more about the incident. It seems that Harlan Davis was cutting hay in back of the house and discovered a big hole in the field. After hearing Joseph Jr.'s report, Joseph Kempkes Sr., then deputy fire chief of the Belchertown Fire Department, decided to contact Westover Field. The air force was using Quabbin Reservoir as a bombing range during the war and it was suspected that this might be a bomb. A team came out from Westover and gingerly began excavation. After they hit metal, they went even more slowly until it was determined it was a practice bomb and was filled with sand. Mr. Kempkes stated that the person excavating the bomb said that the plane must have been flying above two thousand feet as determined by the depth of the crater. As to when it happened and how it happened, no one knows.

An aerial view of Belchertown center.

The air force started using Quabbin Reservoir in 1941 for bombing practice. In a later *Sentinel* article about the use of the reservoir, it said that Quabbin was not yet filled and there were still large areas of cleared land, which "was some distance from habitation." The article went on to say, "The areas now consist of cleared land, but as the reservoir fills, the terrain will be under water, interspersed here and there with small islands. This will make for added safety, as it is probable that targets will be set up on these islands for the bombing planes and isolation will increase the control which will be a mandatory practice." Night bombing practice was started in late autumn in 1942. An article from the *Ware River News* told the people not to be disturbed if they heard many planes going over town in the night hours. "Bombing practice more or less calls for approach to targets from various directions, etc., and that means more flying for many miles around."

A number of planes crashed in Belchertown during the war and heroic rescues were made by its citizens. That is another story. But stories from the pages of the *Sentinel* like the bomb dropping on North Main Street give people today glimpses of what was happening on the home front in Belchertown. I have compiled three large notebooks from the *Sentinel* files, starting in 1939—when Bob Jackson started writing in his column about what was happening in Europe—to 1949. The pages chronicle how Belchertown citizens met the war effort both by serving in the military and on the home front. These notebooks are available for inspection at the Stone House Museum.

Doris Dickinson

BAGGS' BUS SERVICE

The archives of the Stone House Museum contains bits and pieces of Belchertown history in its collection of ephemera—a term used to embrace a wide range of minor, everyday documents, originally intended for one time or short time use. These include a school program, a menu from the Belchertown Inn, tickets for the Police Association dance in Lawrence Memorial Hall, a sale at Hopkins Store and flyers for events sponsored by the many town organizations. Individually, they may have had a short life, but these pieces of printed paper can bring the past to life more vividly that any other form of documentation.

Such was the case several weeks ago. A small piece of red cardboard was given to me by Paul Cook. It read: "Schedule, Baggs' Bus Line between Belchertown, Granby and Holyoke." Fares were fifty cents each way, with stops in Granby. The little card also advertised, "Supplies purchased and Produce Marketed. Errands of all Kinds.

Special Trips at any time." You could leave the Belchertown post office (when it was located on the corner of Maple and Main Street, I imagine) at 7:30 a.m. and arrive at Holyoke City Hall at 8:15 a.m. There was another trip to Holyoke at 10:30 a.m., with a return trip leaving Holyoke at 1:15 p.m. The last bus left Belchertown at 4:00 p.m., leaving Holyoke at 6:00 p.m. for the return trip. There was an extra trip on Saturdays, Sundays and holidays, leaving Belchertown at 7:00 p.m. and returning at 9:00 p.m. This was quite a convenience during those early days when not everyone had an automobile, and the bus made it easier to run errands and take produce to market.

Who was the owner of this bus line and when was it in operation? When I receive such an intriguing item, it starts me searching, mostly in the old *Sentinel*. I found the information in the April 2, 1915 issue. This was the first regular issue of the paper, which had not been named, yet. The masthead read, "Belchertown's Weekly Newspaper," stating that its name would appear next week. But in this first issue I found, under town items, a small one-sentence statement, "M.C. Baggs has bought a new fifteen passenger auto-bus which he will run between Holyoke and Belchertown, beginning about April 15." That sentence had answered both my questions.

The April 23 issue, with its new masthead, had an advertisement that the bus line would start operation on April 26 with a seven-passenger touring car. The fifteen-passenger autobus would be ready about May 1. In the December 24 issue, the line was offering round trip fares of seventy-five cents between Belchertown and Holyoke. The line had just put into commission "at considerable expense, a beautiful enclosed body insuring your comfort and warmth on these cold days."

They also advertised they were prepared to carry parties of from one to twenty-five anywhere at any time at reasonable rates. "Picnic parties, theater parties, trips to Mountain Park, Riverside, Forest Lake, Boston, New London, New York or any place you wish to go, and the larger the party the less the fare per person."

Baggs' Garage was already in business on Everett Avenue and advertising in the first issue of the *Sentinel*. They had Fisk tires, Ford auto parts and Stewart horns. They offered vulcanizing, general repairing, machine work, pipe and pipe fittings, pumps, engines, water systems, etc. Later on, they sold Overland cars.

It isn't clear when the bus line went out of business. In the 1920 census, Milton Baggs is listed as in the automobile business. In the 1930 census, he is listed as being in the hardware business. At some point, Milton C. Baggs focused on plumbing and the installation of heating systems and left the automobile business and bus transportation to someone else.

Many will remember him as the chief of the Belchertown Fire Department. He was appointed in 1925 and served twenty-five years, retiring in 1950. He also served as water commissioner and sewer commissioner during the department's early formation. He died in 1973. I remember him as a very quiet man who could be depended on if one needed help. He contributed to the progress of the community where he lived all the days of his life.

Schedule

Baggs' Bus Line

BETWEEN

Belchertown, Granby and

Holyoke

FARES

Holyoke to Granby Road		10c
"	Five Corners	15c
"	Granby	25c
"	Forge Pond	35c
"	Belchertown	50c

Trunks 25c

Supplies Purchased and Produce Marketed.   Errands of all Kinds. Special Trips at any time.

Orders may be telephoned to Bardwell's Drug Store, Holyoke Tel. 1014 or Baggs' Garage, Belchertown, Tel. 40-2.

The schedule for Baggs' Bus Line, circa 1920s.

A small piece of red cardboard printed, I am sure, by Lewis Blackmer over seventy years ago and given away to customers or left on the counters of local stores, has a great story to tell. Did someone ride that bus to work each day in Holyoke? Maybe someone took the Saturday evening bus to see those early movies. I wonder if a party got together and went to Mountain Park.

When I came to Belchertown almost sixty years ago, the Holyoke Street Railway came to Belchertown and even went to Ware. It was my transportation to both those towns since I did not drive. But it too has faded away.

Doris Dickinson

AN EARLY GIFT TO THE STONE HOUSE MUSEUM

The issues of the *Sentinel* furnish present-day historians with a wealth of information about what was happening in town. Lewis Blackmer had an editorial style that combined news with history. Such was an article that appeared in the May 27, 1927 issue. With the headline "Donor Announced," the article described a gift to the Belchertown Historical Association, which had recently opened the Stone House Museum to the public:

> *Most any town, or city for that matter, would not be what it is today were it not for the thoughtfulness and generosity of those who spent their early years amid its surroundings. Necessity or opportunity has beckoned elsewhere, but affection for the childhood home increases with the years and only waits appropriate expression. Belchertown has been very fortunate in this regard, and names are still being added to those who have laid gifts at our door by reason of this homing spirit. The announcement that Gaston Plantiff has made possible the fence to the south and west of the Stone House furnishes but another illustration of this fact. And it all comes about so naturally, too, as genuine gifts do.*

Mr. Plantiff had made a visit to the Stone House in the fall of the previous year and Mrs. Leila Curtis, custodian of the Stone House, had remarked in passing that she hoped someday the organization would be able to enclose the Stone House with a picket fence. Evidently, Mr. Plantiff offered to render this service and in correspondence with the clerk said, "I have the interests of Belchertown at heart always, and want to do my share to make it attractive and the kind of a town that we all want."

And who was Gaston Plantiff? All are long gone who would remember him or his family. He was born in the brick house on Jabish Street below the service station and attended local schools. He was only sixteen years of age when he left Belchertown to go to work as an office boy at Waltham Watch Factory. There he continued his studies at night school and later entered the employ of the Orient Bicycle Company of Waltham. In connection with his work in the bicycle factory, he entered many of the bicycle races of that day and was the winner of a large number of trophies. Later he went to New York where he was a demonstrator of bicycles for Wanamaker and where he met Henry Ford. He had the distinction of being the first salesman whom Mr. Ford hired and of being in charge of the first salesroom which Mr. Ford opened. When he retired in the early 1930s, he was Ford's New England district manager.

The Stone House Museum with its original fence.

Gaston Plantiff did not forget his hometown, along whose streets he had once been a newsboy. The town is indebted to him for interesting Henry Ford in the Belchertown Historical Association, an interest that resulted in the gift of the Ford Annex on the grounds of the Stone House Museum. Following a visit to the museum, Mr. Ford made a gift of $5,000 to erect the annex. A headline of a *Boston Globe* article proclaimed, "Mr. Ford Falls in Love with Belchertown Antiques, Too," when the gift was announced. At the dedication of the annex in June of 1924, Mr. Plantiff represented Mr. Ford.

Gaston Plantiff died in October of 1934. Mr. Ford made one more visit to Belchertown for his funeral. Bob Jackson in his "Soliloquies of a Steeple" column had this to say: "Last week when he returned to the old home town, the most prominent businessman in America left his work in Detroit to travel here and pay his final respects to this same boy, his friend and former associate in the world's most successful automobile business. Gaston Plantiff had gone far since the days when he had sold the *Republican* to the householders around the Common." Gaston Plantiff is buried in Mount Hope Cemetery.

In the coming months, townspeople will have the opportunity to also show their interest in preserving what is one of the outstanding landmarks in Belchertown. In observance of the hundredth anniversary of the Belchertown Historical Association, a campaign will be launched to install a new picket fence around the Stone House Museum.

Doris Dickinson

THE CANNON AND THE DISAPPEARING CANNONBALLS

Civil War monuments with Union soldiers facing south are fixtures on many commons throughout New England. Sometimes there is a cannon, also facing south. Belchertown is no exception. The story about the Civil War monument has been told in the *Sentinel* over the past few months and events seeking funds for "Sam's" restoration have received a great deal of attention. But the cannon, erected in 1906, also has a story to tell.

The cannon was originally installed on the Common at the instigation of the Grand Army of the Republic (GAR). The story goes that the GAR had always wanted a cannon to go with the monument, which was erected in 1885. A letter written by Mrs. Cornelia Holland and published in the *Belchertown Sentinel* in May 1933, provides a glimpse into its history:

> *Mr. David Shumway said the Grand Army had always wanted a cannon on the common, but had no funds to place it there. He said to me, "Would you go ahead and raise the money to defray expenses if I can get one?" He wrote to Congressman Gillette and he replied that the only one of the size we could handle was in one of the Western States and if we wanted it, he would deliver it free of charge to the Belchertown station. I consulted the Grange and the [Women's] Relief Corps and with their aid planned a supper, the Grange giving the use of the hall. We raised about 40 dollars. If I remember rightly, Dwight Shumway and George Akers with their horses took it from the station to the common and drew the stone for the foundation—all as a gift. Mr. Spencer put in the foundation at a reduced rate. I think Mr. Claflin put up the balls at a cost of five dollars and at that time there was a pile at each corner.*

Her memory was right on target, for newspaper clippings in the Springfield papers chronicled the story over the summer of 1906. One clipping said that the cannon had arrived at the railroad station and would be brought to the village probably soon. Another said, "The cannon was brought to the Common today and is somewhat smaller than it was supposed to be, but when mounted it will be much more imposing. It will point toward the south when in position." Another article was more critical:

> *The much talked of piece of ordnance that was presented to Belchertown by the Government has at last found its resting place. The size of the gun is quite disappointing to the people, who expected to see a large affair, believing that cannons were all large, because they are said to have "volleyed and thundered."*

Spring

Like all new things which disappoint the expectations of some people, there have been many remarks that savored of criticism, as the effect is rather disappointing, now that the cannon is mounted. Some of the people criticize the form of the carriage on which it rests. This is made of cobblestone cast in cement. Previous to putting up the stone carriage, the foundations were put in and much work has been done to get the gun mounted. It is understood that a patriotic meeting will be held to dedicate the new field piece and after this is done and the history of it is known, the people will better understand what it is.

There was a dedication on September 30, 1906. Congressman Frederick Gillette was on hand to make the presentation and gave an address. He presented the gun to Selectman Nelson Randall, who in turn presented it to O.K. Shumway, commander of the GAR. A chorus from the high school sang "Columbia, Gem of the Ocean" and "Nearer, My God, to Thee." The audience sang "America" and Miss Frances Fletcher gave a reading. Thus ended the first chapter of the cannon on the Common.

The cannon and cannon balls guard Belchertown Common under the watchful eyes of the Civil War soldier. Note the old flagpole, which was once a ship's mast.

In her letter, Mrs. Holland mentioned the installation of a pile of cannonballs at each corner of the cannon. Her letter had been prompted by a comment in Bob Jackson's "Soliloquies of the Steeple" about the "loose" cannonballs. Since their installation in 1906, they had been a tempting target. She ends her letter with the following: "Now it looks to me as if the town of Belchertown is the one to keep their property in good condition and either reset the balls or pick them up every day instead of the last GAR man."

In November of 1967, an article in the *Sentinel* heralded the return of the cannon to the Common. It had been removed the previous year when it became loose and stored in the town barn for safekeeping. "People have missed it, wondered idly whether vandals had made off with it, in the same way that the cannonballs have disappeared, but nobody seems to have been greatly concerned over its removal from the common." The American Legion Post 239 resolved to see what could be done about having it replaced. Sidney Wheeler, with the help of Victor Patenaude and then-Highway Superintendent Joseph Kulig, saw to the return of the cannon, which was mounted securely on its base once more and sporting a fresh coat of paint contributed by Isaac Hodgen.

Upon its return, Bob Jackson commented that he was glad to see the cannon back in its place:

> *Without it, the foundation was rather sad. Now all is shipshape again and will remain so until someone else decides to pit his strength against the helpless gun. Pointing south, just as the soldier behind it is facing, the ensemble recalls a past which has never been forgotten. The two small pyramids of cannon balls which originally flanked the cannon were temptations from the start and are long gone. Someone was always tugging away at them. They were useful for amateur shot puts and the like.*

The whereabouts of all the missing cannonballs will probably remain a mystery, but a few still remain. Reposing in the Ford Annex at the Stone House Museum are seven of the original cannonballs. Someone at some point in time past must have made the decision that the museum would be a safe place to preserve these bits of history. When you are on the Common next time, take a look at the venerable old cannon that has stood there for almost a hundred years. Then, stop by at the Stone House Museum where the remaining cannonballs will be on display.

Doris Dickinson

MEMORIAL TREES ON THE COMMON

The *Sentinel* featured a story several weeks ago on a project started by Ann Pittsley, administrative assistant to the board of selectmen, to replace the trees that were being removed around the town center. She probably didn't realize she was carrying on a tradition started many years ago. One Sunday in 1850, Reverend Samuel Wolcott of the Congregational church, preached a sermon on "the Cedars of Lebanon," urging the improvement of the Common. The next day, Reverend Wolcott, with his shovel, gathered a large force of men and began to work. Many trees were set on the east side of the Common and also some trees were planted along South Main Street. I wonder if any of those trees are still standing.

Perhaps the next effort to plant trees on the Common came about in the formation of the Park Association. At a town meeting in 1873, the town approved four resolutions giving the Park Association control of the Common. One of those resolutions gave the group permission "at its own expense to enclose the Common with a fence, set out shade and ornamental trees, and otherwise improve and beautify the Common." The association continued to care for the Common for almost seventy-five years until it was dissolved in May 1947 when the town took back the responsibility. When I came to town in the early 1940s, the association still had their Common Cleanup Day—on or near April 19—when townspeople gathered to rake and beautify.

In 1940 the Park Association ordered nine trees to be set out on the Common and, in addition, individuals and organizations ordered nineteen more, making twenty-eight in all. Among the purchasers were the Belchertown Historical Association, the Clapp Memorial Library and the Gold and Fuller estates. Bob Jackson, in his "Soliloquies of the Steeple" column, had this to say at the time: "Much credit for the spirit of beautification must be given to Park Association President Herman C. Knight, who is tirelessly seeking to make Belchertown a more lovely place in which to live." Mr. Knight was also superintendent of schools. His great-grandson Edward Knight carried on that tradition when he spearheaded the campaign to restore the Civil War monument on the Common.

In 1943 the Park Association set out two memorial trees. One was planted on the west side of the Common across from the Methodist church. This memorial tree, given by the Witt family, was to honor Edgar C. Witt, believed to have been the first road superintendent appointed by the town in the 1890s. He was a former selectman and longtime member of the Methodist church. The other memorial tree was planted on the east side, in proximity to the Congregational church, in memory of the Stebbins family. The tree was given by Miss Nellie Moore of Greenfield, Massachusetts. Miss Moore was the fourth generation descendant of Benjamin Stebbins who came to Cold Spring in July 1731. He remained here throughout his life and raised a family, dying in 1789. The Stebbins family was one of the first to make a permanent settlement here.

In reporting the planting of these trees, the *Sentinel* wrote, "A diagram is to be made by the Park Association, on which will be designated these memorial trees, for future record." Where is that record today? It would let us know if those trees are still on the Common. The only information about the Park Association that I have found comes from early newspaper clippings and, after 1915, the pages of the *Belchertown Sentinel*. I hope that the locations of the new memorial trees will be well-documented in the records of the town for future historians.

Memorial trees were also planted on the Common in honor of the Belchertown men who died during World Wars I and II. In the May 17, 1946 *Sentinel*, there was an article about the Park Association meeting with the American Legion, whose members wanted to plant memorial trees for those who had lost their lives in World War II. A year later, on April 18, 1947, a short article appeared in the *Sentinel* stating that the American Legion would plant ten memorial trees on the Common. In the following week's issue, after meeting with an expert from the Massachusetts State College (now the University of Massachusetts), it was decided to plant the trees "within the present line of trees with five on each side and leave the end open for future planting." These trees were to form a group with the four trees that had been planted in memory of the World War I casualties.

The Common.   Belchertown, Mass.

A postcard view of Belchertown Common.

The World War II trees were in memory of Arthur Barry, James L. Beaudry, Robert T. Dyer Jr., Gilbert T. Geer, Adelphis R. Germain, Francis P. Kulig, Clarence Lamson, James L. Lyon, Donald H. Sessions and Edward Stolar. The World War I casualties were Francis Carew, George Hannum, Chauncey D. Walker and Warren B. Wright.

There are six trees in the line of maples still standing on the Common. The sixth is in memory of Raymond Dahlgren, who lost his life in the Korean War. The other five trees planted on the Park Street side of the Common are no longer standing. Across from the Old Town Hall on Park Street is a large tree that could be one of those planted for the World War I casualties. A second large tree stands in a line in the middle of the Common. David Hodgen said there used to be two more trees in that line.

According to the late Edward Lofland, there is a plaque at the American Legion Hall for Chauncey Walker that used to stand before one of the World War I trees. There were similar plaques for the other World War I casualties. Here lies one of Belchertown's mysteries. What happened to the other plaques? David Hodgen remembers seeing them years ago inside the bandstand. Several World War II veterans that I spoke with remember planting the trees on the Common. There used to be American Legion plaques for holding flags in front of each tree. Although there is no mention of a formal dedication of the trees in the *Sentinel*, one veteran recalls that there was such a ceremony. There was also no mention of what kind of tree was planted.

Doris Dickinson

WILLIAM SQUIRES'S MEMORIAL DAY TRIBUTE

Another Memorial Day has come and gone. Graves have been decorated and speeches have been made. The Union soldier atop the Civil War monument has observed the one hundred and nineteenth ceremony held on the old Belchertown Common since the monument was erected in 1885.

About thirty years ago, the late William Squires, a town selectman from 1964 to 1976, wrote a column for the *Sentinel* entitled "From the Middle Chair." He died in December 1987. His last column ranged far and wide. He was an individual who stood up for what he believed, writing about local, state and national issues. If he took the controversial side of an issue, he did so without malice toward the other side. Bill was a lifelong resident, serving in the U.S. Navy during World War II and the Korean conflict. He owned Squires Garage on Main Street and was a member of the volunteer fire department, a deacon of the Congregational church and one of the first teachers appointed at the opening of Pathfinder Vocational School.

Bill was a great historian, particularly interested in Belchertown history. His column in May 1971 was about his own family history and opened with these words:

> *With the approaching of Memorial Day, I thought I might share a page of family history with you and show you that Memorial Day can be a real day of memory.*
>
> *My great-grandfather (Emory Squires) was the youngest of five brothers. He was too young to serve in the Civil War, but at least two of his brothers did. At that time, it was not called the Civil War, but the War of the Rebellion. Its avowed purpose was to "preserve the Union." This was the culmination of over eighty years of bickering and squabbling among the sovereign states, and was not the first time that states had voted to secede from the Union. Massachusetts had voted to secede from the Union near the close of the War of 1812. But the Civil War was a time of testing of the right to secede and was a statesman's reason for the beginning of hostilities. The people had other and more direct reasons: the abolition of slavery being the main one.*

His great-grandfather's brother, Truman Squires, enlisted as a private on December 21, 1863, at age eighteen. He was mustered in on January 4, 1864 and was killed May 17, 1864, in Spotsylvania, Virginia. Researching at the Clapp Memorial Library, Bill found that Truman was in Company B of the Fifty-seventh Massachusetts Volunteer Infantry, which was in the first brigade of the first division of the Ninth Army Corps.

> *Finding this much information readily available, I decided to pursue the story further. Spotsylvania was one little part in the grand epic called the Battle of the Wilderness. This battle took place in the wooded country of Northern Virginia where neither army could maneuver well because of the dense woods.*

Pursuing a set of volumes at the local library called "The War of the Rebellion, Official Records," he learned that the Fifty-seventh consisted mostly of veterans and had left from Worcester on April 18, 1864, and arrived at Annapolis on April 20. On April 23, they started marching for Washington, the Fifty-seventh Massachusetts being one of the lead units. On the afternoon of April 25, the unit was reviewed by President Lincoln and General Burnside, crossed the Potomac and encamped near Arlington. The first battle in which they were engaged was on May 6 along the Plank Road between Orange and Fredericksburg. Losses were quite

The Civil War statue, now known as "Sam," vigilantly faces south.

heavy. The Fifty-seventh lost 47 killed, 161 wounded and 43 missing. From this time on the Fifty-seventh was always close to the battle, sometimes in a supporting role. Rain began on May 12 and continued until the seventeenth. On May 12, the Fifty-seventh was engaged near Spotsylvania Court House and lost 13 killed, 55 wounded and 4 missing. "I presume Truman died of wounds from this battle."

The final paragraph of his column, written over thirty years ago during Vietnam, seems appropriate today:

> *And men still die in the mud and the blood trying to get possession of some obscure piece of real estate, and for some reason that seems senseless to half the population. But this only happens after all the talk and discussion has proved futile. Memorial Day is a tribute to the determination of the men who uphold ideals that statesmen have been forced to compromise or abandon. These ideals are often redeemed only at the price of misery and death.*

Doris Dickinson

Summer

A TALE OF TWO PIKES

T wo years ago, at the Memorial Day services at Quabbin Park Cemetery, I ran into an old acquaintance from the Swift River Valley, Chester King, who told me the following story.

He had to go to Boston and decided to try the Massachusetts Turnpike for the first time. Since he lived in Athol, his usual route would have been via Route 2. So, he headed south and picked up the pike near Worcester. As he approached the gate, he saw the sign that read, "Fast Lane—No Cash." (Remember, Chester had never been on the pike in his life.) That sounded like a good deal to him, so through the gate he went and not much later, he was stopped by a trooper who looked at his papers and perhaps, seeing he was ninety-two years old, took him into custody, leaving his car behind. He was never told why he was stopped and was taken home to Athol by a series of relays from barracks to barracks. He asked what would happen to his car and was assured it would be taken care of. The last relay was driven by a female trooper and he said she was "nice." Not long after, a towing company called and said he could come and get his car. A friend took him and he ransomed his car for seventy-five dollars. Then, soon after that he got a citation in the mail that he must pay a fine of fifty dollars for his violation. He waited too long to pay the fine and they added on five dollars more. Chester decided not to make a fuss about his trouble, for he realized he could lose his license to drive. He has since moved to California to be with one of his children. I hope he doesn't try the freeways.

THE OTHER PIKE

In November, my friend David and I left on a motoring trip to the Southwest to visit a mutual friend who had moved from Belchertown for his health. David had never toured that part of the country. He also wanted to visit Columbia, Missouri, where he had spent several years in his youth. We took advantage of the transponder on our windshield to take us through several turnpikes and bridges without stopping to pay. The Fast Lane pass used on the MassPike is good for the entire East Coast. In Columbia, Dave was thrilled to see his old neighborhood and house in good condition. From there, we continued on to Kansas City and headed for the Kansas Turnpike. As we approached the tollgates, I saw what appeared to be the equivalent of our Fast Lane system. David wasn't sure, but know-it-all Harvey assured him it would be all right. A red light stopped us, but after a few seconds, it turned green. I told David, it just took a little while to do the billing. So, off we went, for the cars were piling up behind us. When we left the tollbooth, David said that the green light was activated by the car behind us. At this point, I figured David was right and we were about to be arrested, or whatever they do with out-of-state miscreants. We kept going—we couldn't turn around and go back.

We traveled for miles and were not stopped. In fact, we went about two hundred miles and proceeded to leave the turnpike where we had planned. We stopped at a tollbooth and explained what we had done and asked how we could make amends. The woman toll collector said that the transponders only work in the state where they are issued. She was wrong, but we were not in any position to argue. She then called on her phone to someone in charge. She laughed a little and asked if we were driving a green Buick. Yes, they had us pegged. She asked us where we got on and we could not give her a coherent answer. Can we pay, we asked, and she said it would be thirty-five cents (yes, thirty-five cents, not dollars). Smiling, she waved us goodbye and said, "Have a nice day." Astounded, David and I agreed that we were indeed, "having a nice day" and the people in Kansas were nice people.

Harvey Dickinson

THE OLD ELM AND THE SEAT OF THE SCORNFUL

The current exhibit at the Stone House Museum features an enlarged photograph of a postcard of Belchertown during the early 1900s. The photograph shows the center of town and the large elm tree that stood in front of the post office at the corner of Main and Maple Streets. Around the trunk of the tree was a bench that provided a resting place. Many generations must have used this spot as they went about their daily business, picking up their mail or shopping in Longley's Store. In later years, they might have had a bite to eat at Garvey's

Lunch or stopped off at Jackson's Store, then owned by John W. Jackson. An early photograph taken by Mr. Jackson shows the tree with Samuel Allen and James H. Davis sitting on the bench. He entitled the photograph "The Old Tree in front of Garvey's with its Seat of the Scornful."

In 1922 the tree was deemed unsafe and was cut down. Lewis Blackmer, editor of the *Sentinel*, had this to say about the event:

> *The historic elm in front of the post office was cut down today by Tree Warden George H. Kelley and a gang of men. The elm was thought to be a menace to nearby buildings as it showed signs of decay. The tree has long been a landmark in the center of town and much regret has been expressed because it was necessary to remove [it]. A bench formerly encircled the tree where the town philosophers used to gather to whittle and talk. The tree also served as a bulletin board until the state law forbidding [the] posting of notices on shade trees was enforced. In short, it formerly served as the town center for news, and the discussion of all the topics, gossip and scandals, real and imaginary, for many years of the town's history. The tree was of value not only for its historical associations, but it added much of beauty to the center of town, and it will be missed by all who are familiar with the village.*

Sam Allen (left) and James H. Davis pass some time at the "seat of the scornful."

Later on, the *Sentinel* noted that tree specialists had inspected the butt log of the elm and deemed it to be between 250 and 350 years old: "Working up the trunk of the tree is going to present some difficulties not only account of its immense size but also because an armor plate of nails and tacks has been left imbedded in the tree by those who have posted bills and notices there for over a century."

If that age estimate is true, that venerable elm must have been standing alongside the trail that men traveled on horseback and foot between Northampton and Brookfield. This trail later became the Northampton and Boston Stage Road. This road passed by a spring that later gave the area its first name, Cold Spring, before its incorporation as Belcher's Town in 1761. What stories that old tree could have told as the history of the town unfolded around it through the years. The *Sentinel* reported, "Few trees are awarded the honor of so much attention at the time of their decease."

Doris Dickinson

MARJORIE TILTON

A woman sitting on the board of selectmen seems a common sight now, but this was not always the case. Before the election of 1945, no woman had ever served on the board. In 1945, history was made when Mrs. Marjorie G. Tilton took out nomination papers and won a seat. She became the first woman to try for a seat and to crash the board of selectmen in Belchertown. Mr. Lewis Blackmer, then editor of the *Sentinel* said, "Few new male candidates ever make the board on the first try."

Evidently, some people even questioned whether she could run. The *Sentinel* also published a paid ad from Mrs. Tilton that stated: "Excerpt from—General Laws, Commonwealth of Massachusetts—Chapter 41, Sec. 1, page 17, which stated: 'Women shall be eligible to all town offices, notwithstanding any special law to the contrary.'"

Bob Jackson, commenting in his Steeple column, had his usual overview about the election:

> *It was an encouraging election for the more recently emancipated sex. Marjorie Tilton crashed into a triangle held firmly by men since the town was founded. Somehow I don't particularly envy Marjorie. To find oneself a precedent must be a little scary...But don't be a silent partner, Mrs. Tilton. Let it be said later that not only was the first female candidate for the office of selectman elected, but also was an excellent member of triumvirate.*

Marjorie Buss Tilton.

Serving on the board with her were veteran members Charles Austin and Dr. Francis Austin. Terms on the board then were for one year. Town government was centered in two offices in Lawrence Memorial Hall—one for the selectmen and one for the town clerk. They met in the selectmen's room, which is now the office of the veterans' agent, on Friday evenings from eight until ten o'clock. A new innovation was instituted that year. They decided that each member would assume the responsibility of overseeing a town department. Mrs. Tilton became chairman of the board of welfare.

Running again in 1946, she was the top vote-getter in the Republican caucus and received the second highest vote in the election and served a second term. She was on the board during the Welcome Home Celebration on July 4, 1946, for returning veterans of World War II. After serving two terms, she chose not to run for a third term.

During her last year, Mrs. Tilton opened a gasoline station and restaurant on Route 9 known as Tilton's Sunoco Service Station, later as Tilton and Johnston Restaurant. By winning a seat on the board in 1945, Marjorie Tilton, in today's language, "crashed through the glass ceiling" and opened the way for others. Since then, seven women have served: Eleanor Schmidt, 1969–72; Joanne Newman, 1982–88; Pauline Johnson, 1988–91; Florine Neggers, 1996–99; and Linda Barron, who was elected in 1988 and has served for eighteen years.

Doris Dickinson

THE BLACKSMITH SHOP

My better half, Doris, spends time on the Web with an eye on eBay, searching for ephemera, postcards and the like, looking for things related to Belchertown. Not long since, she topped the bid on a trade card for the old blacksmith shop on South Main Street. Old trade cards are the equivalent of today's business cards. One has to be getting along, as they say, to remember the old shop that stood between the second and third house past the Clapp Library. My family home was directly across from the library.

I remember the ring of Bert Shaw's hammer on the anvil as he shaped a horseshoe. South Main Street in the early 1930s was not paved. It was a quiet residential way with hardly any traffic, so Bert's hammer oftentimes was the only sound in the neighborhood. The sound would often beckon me to the old shop. Bert would let me turn the crank on the forge blower, but he also took time to show me how to shape and weld pieces of iron together. I was allowed to use the wood-turning lathe to craft a baseball bat. It was a good looking piece of work, but made of maple instead of ash. It was almost too heavy to swing, but I kept it around the house for decades.

Bert was a powerful man, as farriers had to be. Shoeing a large draft horse was no picnic. Picking up the foot of a horse weighing a ton or more and holding its hoof in your lap took nerve and strength. Bert Shaw was also the chief of police and was able to "keep the peace" and "render justice." He never carried a gun or pepper spray. An ax handle would suffice in extreme cases. His "cruiser" was his pickup truck.

In the late 1920s and early 1930s, there was a dance hall on Route 9 in the Holland Glen section of town that seemed to draw quite a few rowdies. Bert and Constable Clarence Bisnette were often called upon to keep the peace. Oftentimes a great brawl would break out, whereupon Bert would fight his way into the middle of the melee, then punch his way out, while Clarence would circle the outside, picking off stragglers with his feet. Clarence had the ability to fight with his feet, a sort of primitive but effective karate. The brawl was soon over and peace once again reigned at Holland Glen, albeit with a few bloody noses and missing teeth.

Herbert Curtis had retired and rented the shop to Bert. Herb was quite sure of himself and, at times, would tell Bert how things should be done. There was a time that Bert had a chance to show Herb that he was not always right. My father had a cow staked out in Herb's backyard next to the shop. It so happened that the cow calved there. (Back then, a cow substituted for a lawn mower in many cases.) Herb came into the shop to announce to Bert the birth of a heifer calf and went back in his house. It so happened that one of Bert's cows had earlier had a bull calf that was marked very like our heifer calf. Bert jumped into his truck and brought his bull calf and swapped it, hiding our calf in the shop privy. When Herb next appeared,

Bert got onto him about not being able to tell the difference between a heifer and a bull. After that, Herb was less inclined to offer his opinion on things, for Bert could always bring up the "calf incident."

There was a small living quarter in one corner of the shop where a man named Fred Nooney lived. He was a kind of "jack of all trades" and often helped Bert. One summer afternoon in 1936, Herb Story, the paperboy, handed Fred the *Daily News*. Fred looked at the headline announcing the abdication of King Edward "for the woman he loved," Wallis Simpson. Fred slammed the paper to the ground, yelling "He gave up a Kingdom for a [unprintable]." Fred was more of a practical than a romantic type.

GO TO

MR. CURTIS' SHOP,

FOR

HORSESHOEING,

AND

REPAIRING.

A trade card for Curtis' Blacksmith Shop.

The ring of an anvil may have inspired Giuseppe Verde's Anvil Chorus scene in his opera *Il Trovatore*. Some of my contemporaries must remember the music, but I looked up an outline of the opera on the Web. The Anvil Chorus scene depicts Spanish gypsies striking their anvils at dawn and singing the praises of hard work, good wine and their gypsy women. I'll drink to that—and to the music of Bert's anvil from the blacksmith shop on South Main Street many summers ago.

Harvey Dickinson

PARSONS FIELD

Belchertown's recreational fields have been busy this summer and will continue to be during the coming fall school season. It's hard to believe that once upon a time the Common was the only "playing field" for the schools and townspeople and the old town hall was the site for basketball games and physical education. Sometimes, a farmer's field could be used until it was needed for other purposes, but for the most part the Common, unsatisfactory as it was, was used most of the time. The need for a proper playing field was discussed for many years, but little came of the discussion.

In 1938 there appeared in the *Sentinel* a headline, "Recreation Field Assured." And therein lies the beginning of Belchertown's first recreational site—Parsons Field. Mr. Lawrence "Shep" Parsons was born in Belchertown, August 3, 1854, the son of Thomas J.S. and Margaret A. (Weston) Parsons. His father was one of the carriage manufacturers of Belchertown and his mother came from one of the oldest families in town. He was educated in the local schools, being a member of the first class to complete the four-year course in the newly established high school. As a young man, he entered the railroad business and worked in Louisville, Kentucky, for over fifty years, later being in charge of transportation for the International Paper Company in New York. Upon retirement, he traveled extensively throughout Europe, Egypt and the Middle East. When he wanted to share his experiences, he would drop a line to the *Sentinel*, which published his letters, giving people a "folksy," sometimes humorous, narrative of places unfamiliar to many.

But in the spring, there was that urge to return to his "hometown," to the old homestead on Main Street. For over fifteen years, the Parsons usually arrived back in Belchertown in May or June and remained until October entertaining their friends and tending a large flower garden on the extensive grounds of their home. One of his favorite pastimes was to lean back in his camp chair under a maple at the north end of the Common on a summer afternoon and root for the amateur hometown ball team and champion its rights when a dispute arose.

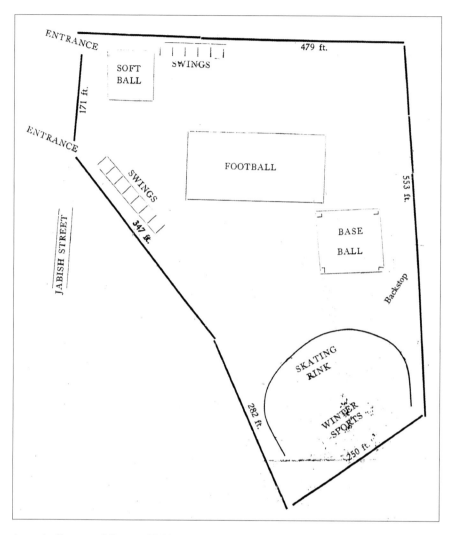

An early diagram of Parsons Field.

Mr. Parsons died on February 21, 1931, at his home in New York, as he was planning to come to Belchertown to visit Dr. George MacPherson, then superintendent of the Belchertown State School. He is buried in Mount Hope Cemetery, just across the Common from his ancestral home at 17 Main Street. Several years later, his daughter, Mrs. Willing Spencer, mentioned to Dr. MacPherson that she would like to provide a fitting memorial for her father. The result is Parsons Field. After looking around for a suitable place, she purchased property from Henry Gould on the corner of Jabish Street and Jensen Road. Work began on the field in June of 1939 and $26,336 was designated by the federal government as a Works Progress Administration project. Curry Hicks, then head of the physical education department at Massachusetts State College, was to give his advice in determining the best location for the baseball diamond. Space was also to be provided for softball and football with a wading pool and ice-skating rink to be added later. Local townspeople were hired to work on the project. Aubrey Lapolice, Lafayette Ayers and Michael Mathras were also involved in the development of the field.

A dedication was held at the field in September 1940, when Mrs. Spencer handed over the deed to the property to Lloyd C. Chadbourne, chairman of the board of selectmen. One of the highlights of the event was the schoolchildren's performance of a song written especially for the occasion by Bob Jackson. The first game was played on the field in May 1941 when Belchertown High School met Petersham in the first game of the season. In connection with the event, there was a flag raising ceremony and Charles F. Austin, chairman of the selectmen tossed out the ball in big league fashion. This was a memorable afternoon in Belchertown history. There wasn't a tree in sight and a ball had to travel close to four hundred feet from home plate to reach the center field wall.

The recreation department now uses fields at the state school, high school, Chestnut Hill and Cold Spring Schools, as well as the Austin/Gaughan Field, and a new field is being developed on Sargent Street and will be a memorial to the late Ron Constantino.

The next time you go down Jabish Street to Parsons Field, take a look at the bronze tablet that was set in the stone wall near the entrance, bearing the inscription "Lawrence Parsons Memorial Field, 1939." While you are there, think of Shep Parsons sitting on the Common and cheering on the home team.

Doris Dickinson

SCRUB ON THE COMMON

Somewhere in the torrent of electioneering verbiage of the last presidential election was heard the sound bite "soccer mom," and the phrase has now become part of our everyday language. Everyone was talking about the many hours each week a modern-day mother spends carpooling her kids and their friends to organized sports activities. Soccer, baseball, hockey, basketball, football—all these games are now well organized and run by adults. Uniforms, sponsors, coaches, umpires and managers are involved. Mom is kept on the run hauling kids to practice and games.

A baseball game at the north end of Belchertown Common, circa 1940.

When I was young, we had few organized games and soccer was a strange game that was played by kids in Ludlow, where a large portion of the population was of Portuguese descent. Soccer was a popular sport played around the world, but was not a big sport in the United States until lately. When I was in high school there was an attempt to establish an interest in soccer, but it never caught on. Of course, back then the popular game was baseball.

We had a form of baseball we called "scrub" that we played on summer afternoons and evenings at the south end of the Belchertown Common where the parking lot is now. There was no marked diamond and the bases were most anything handy—perhaps a piece of cardboard from the First National Store across the street or a convenient rock in the grass—but by the time summer was over, we had a well-defined base path worn into the turf. Age meant nothing, whether you were six or sixteen, you could join the game. Play could begin with four or five players; pitcher, catcher, first baseman, infielder/outfielder and batter. As more players arrived and all the infield positions were filled, newcomers had to start in the outfield and there was no limit to the number of players, but you had to remember your place in the rotation. The role of the pitcher was merely to toss the ball to where the batter could hit it. The catcher's job was a passive one, just to return the ball to the pitcher. Base runners were not allowed to steal bases, but could only advance on a fair ball. The batter was allowed three strikes, but could choose the pitch he wanted. If he got a hit, he was on his own, for the following batters had no responsibility to a base runner. Every batter and runner was on his own and, if a runner got home safely, he could bat again. If he struck out or was put out on the bases, he had to go to the outfield and wait his turn to bat again. The catcher would then bat, the pitcher would become the catcher, the first baseman would pitch and each position would move up. Any player catching a fly ball would be the next one up. The score was not kept, for there was no team play; it was the batter against all the other players.

In the evening, we quit playing when we could no longer see the ball. This was a game for all age groups without coaches, umpires, schedules or parents on the sidelines. There were no winners or losers and each player got to play all positions. The little kids were often allowed to stay at bat until they hit the ball and were given breaks on running. Perhaps this game was like the "stickball" that city kids played in the street.

In the fall, we played touch football as they do today on the open parts of the Common. Regular baseball games—that is, the high school and town teams—were played on the north end of the Common. The foul lines ran through the trees along the edge of the Common and across the road. Everything was in play. Dodging cars in the street added excitement to the game. The players didn't mind because the ground rules applied to each side.

One summer, we kids organized a team that we called the Belchertown Wildcats. We had no sponsor or help from "mom," but we challenged a bunch of boys in South Belchertown and played in the field opposite Keyes Hotel, now the Winthrope House. One of the local school bus drivers agreed to transport us. He cheered us on, with the aid of the hotel's beer tap, from the porch of the hotel that overlooked the field. When the game was mercifully over—we were drubbed by an obscene score—our bus driver was nowhere to be seen. Maybe he didn't think we deserved a ride home, so we walked the seven or more miles home, cursing the bus driver and grumbling over the humiliating loss. No one called his parents for a ride home. Most likely, the fathers would have been at work with the family car.

We also played a primitive game of hockey back then, when a section of the north end of the Common was flooded by the firemen. Another favorite place to skate was Spencer's Pond on Jensen Road, a little way beyond South Cemetery. It was not much more than a couple of acres in size, but it froze earlier than the lakes.

Even after Parsons Field was completed in 1940, we continued to use the south end of the Common as a sports playground, until it was paved for a parking lot. Driving around town you now see playing fields everywhere. The town, as it has grown, has added more and more recreational fields to accommodate the needs of our growing population. The Common is still used for many events, but the time of scrub baseball there on long summer evenings has passed.

Harvey Dickinson

FOURTH OF JULY CELEBRATIONS

T he Fourth of July is just around the corner. Strawberries are ripe for picking, green peas will soon be on the market and the corn seems to be, according to an old Yankee saying, "knee high on the fourth of July." The newspapers are full of events to celebrate America's birthday—concerts, fireworks and parades are on order in many of the surrounding towns. Belchertown, to all appearances, will remain fairly quiet. But this wasn't always the case. Bob Jackson, in a column in 1956, commented on happenings in Belchertown during the early days:

> *Traditionally, from the days of the Revolution up to perhaps twenty years ago, this was the noisiest of our celebrations. Starting at dusk on July 3 and continuing until all the kids (young and old) were out of ammunition, the quietness of this hilltop and all American hamlets and cities the length and breadth of the land, was rocked by explosions, major and minor.*

Americans gradually got tired of all the noise and, maybe more so, of the danger. State by state, the sale of fireworks was banned. But as late as July 1936, E.C. Howard and D.D. Hazen advertised they would be selling fireworks on the end of the Common:

> *Along with the amateur use of explosives, our old Fourths were memorable for a "Night Before" celebration that featured bell ringing, bonfires, and considerable hell-raising. It was like Halloween is now, to some extent, but was confined to one night, and there were other differences. The stroke of midnight from the Old Town Clock was the signal here in Belchertown for starting the bonfire and ringing the bells at the church and the old High School...The bonfire was the pride of certain "older young men" who strove each year to make the pile higher and more spectacularly combustible than any of the famous towers of the past. For days before, collections of wooden boxes and barrels were made from the grocery stores and other business houses, along with old lumber, discarded wooden vehicles— anything that could be piled and burned. Possibly one reason for the present lack of bonfires is the scarcity of the sort of materials from which they used to be made—where could one find wooden packing boxes and barrels today?*

The materials were brought to the "square" off the south end of the Common about ten o'clock. The constables would block off traffic from that vicinity. "The pile was constructed with loving care and considerable risk to necks and legs. By eleven o'clock, it stood, a hundred feet or more in circumference and thirty or forty feet in height."

To a small boy, this was a lovely combination of sight and sound—the crackling and roar of the big fire, ringed by worried firemen; the harsh melody of the bells, now transformed from summonses to dull school or solemn church to patriotic announcements of the Birth of Independence; and the whambango of fireworks, tossed about with largesse and abandon. The "Night Before" was chaos and abandon. It was legalized bedlam, the like of which no boy could ever forget. It was part of his heritage…A small boy surely got a kick out of that night, and it stands out like the Fair, as a highlight in my circling years.

There was even a song about the "Night Before the Fourth," he recalled:

We'll put the pig in the parlor. We'll put the pig in the parlor.
We'll put the pig in the par-aa-arr-lorr.
The Night Before the Fourth.
We won't go home until morning. We won't go home until morning,
We won't go home until mo-oo-oorn-ing
The Night Before the Fourth.

And there were evidences of the night to be seen when the sun rose over the Quabbin Hills. A buggy might be perched atop the bandstand, or an effigy of some unpopular local or national character might be dangling from the arm of one of the lampposts…Sometimes there were "patriotic exercises," with a speaker, a band, and a parade. If there had been an appropriation, or if there was a generous citizen with a large lawn, there might be a fireworks display to round out the holiday.

Bob recalled that despite the side attractions, the old Fourths concentrated on the reason behind the celebration, and with the reading of the Declaration of Independence. "Our attention was focused once a year on the significant fact that Belchertown was once a colonial town, whose residents were subjects of a far-off king and that those ancestors of ours decided upon independence and began a new life as residents of the United States America."

Happy Fourth of July. Have you read the Declaration of Independence lately?

Doris Dickinson

GEORGE WESTON

Who was George Weston, someone asked? George Weston had been chosen by the board of selectmen and the townspeople to present the newly erected Soldiers' Monument to the E.J. Griggs Post No. 97, Grand Army of the Republic at the dedication held on September 15, 1885. Newspaper accounts state that between three and four thousand people, including Civil War veterans, gathered that day on the Common for the dedication. Who was George Weston and why was he chosen for the presentation? Was he a veteran? Questions like these always start another research project with a mystery to solve.

The Weston family was among the early settlers in the Turkey Hill section of Belchertown. George Boardman Weston, the last of nine children, was born on July 21, 1834, and grew up on the Weston farm on Boardman Road. He was described by local historian Clara Dwight Hazen as having had the "wonderlust [*sic*]" and traveled abroad. Another local historian wrote that he had "spent seven years in different countries of Europe and was an authority on Russian and Turkish affairs in which countries he lived several years." He was a glib speaker and could "entertain an audience as few native sons could."

After his travels, George returned to Belchertown and married Martha Curtis, a daughter of Reverend Moses Curtis of Belchertown. They had two children—a son, Roderick, and an adopted daughter, Stella. George took over the family sawmills and lived in the family homestead, which is still standing. He owned and operated Weston's mills (saw and shingle) and was a manufacturer of and dealer in lumber until the mills burned in 1900. He died in 1909.

Four of his grandchildren are still living: Mildred Weston King of Belchertown, Margaret Weston Arena of Springfield, Robert Weston of Wilbraham and Howard Weston of Granby. Local maps still show a Weston Pond where the mills were located and a Weston Brook.

George Weston was not a veteran. In fact, during that period, he was working for an American company in Sebastopol, helping to raise Russian ships that had been sunk in the Black Sea during the Crimean War. Upon his return to Belchertown at the close of the Civil War, he evidently started giving public lectures about his years in Constantinople and became a popular speaker. Clara Dwight Hazen wrote, "On his return his lectures on Constantinople were in demand and he visited the towns about. He could be seen on our streets, a gentleman to be proud of."

He began writing for the *Springfield Republican* about his travels. The *Republican* printed the following introduction to a series about the raising of the Russian fleet:

Mr. George B. Weston begins in this issue a series of articles descriptive of life in the neighborhood of the Black sea, at the time of the Crimean war, and detailing adventures among the Turks, Russian Tartars, and Cossacks. This series will be found of great interest and value, as an expert of many years in eastern countries entitles the author to be considered an authority upon the topics of which he writes. The first paper is a very graphic narrative of the raising of the Russian war vessels in the Black sea; the next will be entitled "A ride over the Crimean battle-fields."

These little bits of information give clues as to why the town might have picked him to make the presentation, but town records also give evidence that he spoke quite eloquently at the town meetings when the E.J. Griggs Post petitioned the town for funds for the monument. The town voted $850 towards the monument with the stipulation that a matching sum be raised by subscription from the townspeople.

LECTURE
Number Two.

GEORGE B. WESTON,

A Wanderer in many countries,

Will deliver the SECOND LECTURE of his course,

SUBJECT:

TWO YEARS IN CONSTANTINOPLE;
Its Mysteries, Miseries and Splendors.

CONTENTS.

What Constantinople has been formerly—What it is now—Its external Magnificence—The contrast upon landing—Narrow streets—Dilapidated buildings—Different races—The variety of costumes—Turkish Coffee

A poster for a lecture given by George Weston.

Myron Walker, chairman of the dedication, had this to say when introducing Mr. Weston: "He has done much by his pen and voice to secure this monument. He has been the soldiers' friend and we may almost call him comrade. He now crowns all his former personal efforts." A newspaper account of the event said that Mr. Weston spoke in somewhat florid language. He thanked Mr. Walker for alluding to his efforts in town meeting to secure an appropriation for the monument and said that it would be unnatural for anyone to feel otherwise than friendly towards the Griggs Post, "a body of men who formed a component part of the Grand Army, which did so much for the cause of humanity and good government." He told the veterans that "in the future their descendants would surround the monument, notebooks in hand to take from it in the names of great grandsires who served in a war whose Gettysburg and Spotsylvania will be as remote to them as Trenton and Brandywine are to us."

His concluding remarks were almost prophetic. He hoped that "if, in the coming time, the present monument shall corrode and time's effacing fingers mar the glorious names inscribed thereon, another generation, more wealthy and equally patriotic, may replace it with another, more substantial, more deserving, more artistic." Recently, the old monument has been repaired, again through the generosity of many individuals, grants and fundraising events, and should stand, once more, for generations to come.

Doris Dickinson

CRONEY'S CORNER

The intersection of Routes 21 and 202 has seen more changes during the last year than the previous fifty years. Years ago, this area was known as Croney's Corner. Mary "Minnie" Croney owned a restaurant, a tearoom or a roadside stand on this site, depending on who is telling the story.

Mary Sullivan came to this country in 1894 from County Kerry, Ireland. She came to Holyoke where she married Frederick Croney in 1906. They were living in Belchertown when their son, Francis, was born on December 4, 1908. Deed records show that Fred Croney bought the property, "land and buildings thereon," in 1901 from Samuel Allen.

Minnie and her family lived in the small house still standing on the corner. Minnie must have started her business soon after coming to Belchertown. Her obituary stated that she had operated a restaurant for over forty-five years. Many of the older residents of Belchertown have fond memories of going down to Croney's Corner for an ice cream, a soda, a hot dog or hamburger and some even had a cup of tea.

Raymond Gould, on left, delivering groceries at Croney's Corner.

Sherman Gould remembers going down for the five- and ten-cent hot dogs—the ten-cent ones were special, he said. A picture from the Stone House archives shows his father, Raymond Gould, some forty years earlier, delivering groceries at the same corner in front of the house.

Helen Lister, who came to Belchertown to teach at the state school, remembers going over to have a cup of tea. Minnie made very strong tea. Harold LaBroad remembers getting a cup of coffee and using two spoons of sugar and Minnie saying, "Couldn't you use just one?" June Henneman recalls her family taking a Sunday drive and stopping at Minnie's for tea and sandwiches. Nancy Pratt remembers that her favorite ice cream was butter crunch. She said that Minnie used to play whist with Lillian Sears, Peg Austin and Dorothy McKillop.

Andrew Sears, who lives up on Turkey Hill, has many good memories of Croney's Corner. His father was the rural mail carrier in Belchertown and Granby for over thirty-three years and he had a great sense of humor. One day they stopped for ice cream. When asked what flavor, his father said, "Chocoberry." Minnie replied, "What the hell is that?"

Fred Croney painted the Sears's house several times and, like many old-time painters, always mixed the paint himself. Andrew's father would take Minnie to Mass every Sunday. Andrew remembers he and his friend Walter Smola rode their bikes down every Sunday to get ice cream. "It was the thing to do." Minnie had chairs and tables on the lawn in the rear of the stand. He remembers polishing the apples they would bring down from the farm for Minnie to sell.

A gas pump stood just outside the front door of the house. It was the type that you had to crank to pump the gas. Andrew thinks the gas was Socony brand. Minnie had a one-quart glass container with a spout that she used to add oil to your engine. He remembers that she loved to talk, but was a hard worker.

I talked with many people about Croney's Corner and no matter whom I talked with, they all remembered Minnie. Most of the time, the comment was: "She was quite a character." One person remarked that she was as "Irish as Murphy's pig." Another, that she was "sparky and sassy." I am sure there are more people who remember Minnie and have other stories to tell. I only wish I could find a picture of her.

Minnie must have had a good business for a while. The Belchertown State School construction was underway during the 1920s and 1930s and Quabbin Reservoir construction was also drawing people to the area.

Back during the latter part of 1918, articles began to appear with great regularity in the *Belchertown Sentinel* about the fundraising activities of the Catholic Mission. They were in the process of buying the community hall for a church. Mrs. Croney's name was usually listed among those who worked on the various suppers, fairs and entertainments.

Fred Croney was a railroad man for many years and was a member of the Brotherhood of Railroad Trainmen. The 1920 census lists him as a brakeman and the 1930 census lists him as a conductor. He served the town as a member of the board of registrars. Phyllis Root remembers that her father, Cliff Rawson and Mr. Croney were great fishing buddies. They belonged to a group of Belchertown men who had a fishing camp on Pottpaug Pond in Hardwick, now part of Quabbin Reservoir. At his funeral in 1941, most of the pallbearers were members of the Belchertown Fire Department. Fred Croney is buried in Mount Hope Cemetery.

Their son, Francis Croney, attended local schools and in the 1930 census was listed as working on the railroads, as well. He died in 1934 and is buried in Calvary Cemetery in Holyoke.

Mary (Sullivan) Croney died on January 26, 1958, in her home on Croney's Corner and is buried beside her son in Calvary Cemetery in Holyoke.

The story of the Croney family and Croney's Corner is part of Belchertown history—the kind of history that isn't written in history books. It lives in the memories of the people who remember Minnie, her wit, humor and many good works. I remember reading somewhere that a person never really dies as long as they remain in someone's memory.

A new history is in the process of being written for Croney's Corner. Where a tall stand of pine trees once stood, a complex has been erected that contains a bank, medical offices and a gym. Fred and Minnie's house still stands and is being renovated for new tenants. The Footloose dance studio is being erected by Justin and Melissa Martin behind the house on the land that Fred Croney purchased in 1901.

Doris Dickinson

GENE DICK

Towns used to have their "characters." There was something unique about them that made them stand out from the crowd. Belchertown had its share and back in the early 1900s Lucy Thomson, an early historian, wrote an article for the newspaper about some of these early residents. The article didn't degrade these individuals and it made for great reading about their eccentricities. This got me to thinking if I could recall such individuals during the years I have lived in Belchertown. Several came to mind. One that I remember was called "Gene Dick." He was born Eugene Dixon in Belchertown on August 18, 1872, and died in late June 1966, at ninety-four years of age. He had lived most of his life in Belchertown and is buried in Mount Hope Cemetery.

When he died, Bob Jackson wrote in his Steeple column that he had forgotten that Gene's real name was Eugene Dixon and recalled some of his memories:

> *He was a grown man and a "town character" when I was a small boy, and his name has always stood for something in my mind. When I say "town character," I am by no means belittling him. One of my dictionaries defines a "character" as "a person whose behavioral processes are unusual"…The term is used to show either deprecation or a person's eccentricity or affection for a person's individuality. It is such affection that I hail Gene Dick as one of the town's most famous "characters." I remember the amazement I felt as a kid when I first saw him tell time. He drew a large watch from his pocket, snapped open the face-glass, and lightly-touched the hands, with his lips.*

Yes, Gene Dick was blind. His obituary said he had been blind since youth, but stories abound about him and how he dealt with his handicap. I first recall seeing Gene Dick walking up Maple Street from his home on Howard Street with his long cane in hand. While I was working as a clerk in Jackson's Store, he would come in for his cut plug tobacco. There was a machine for cutting off a section—he always ordered a ten-cent piece and would measure it out in his hand just to make sure he got the right amount. One time he came in looking for some tomato plants that someone was to have left for him. I looked everywhere and couldn't find any. He insisted they were there and started waving his cane around. Mr. Jackson came running up and calmed him down and escorted him out of the store before any damage could be done.

I first heard about Gene Dick before I ever came to Belchertown. It seems that he had put an ad in the *Sentinel* in February 1944. It read: "Wanted—a large wash tub or a wife all equipped." This unusual ad got picked up as an interesting bit and showed up in papers all over the country and eventually in *Time* magazine, where my husband, then in the navy in California, heard of it. Lewis Blackmer, editor of the *Sentinel*, later commented on the ad: "We are still getting reverberations from that ad of Gene Dick's…Evidently it got copied all over the country, for friends everywhere have been sending back clippings concerning it. Of course not too many out of town people know that Gene Dick is Belchertown's blind man, full of fun, and that he quickly fell for the suggestion of a friend that he might advertise for a wife all equipped, when he was about to insert an ad for a wash tub." Although no woman answered the ad, we later found out that my husband's father, Howard Dickinson, had given him the washtub.

The *Sentinel* is always a good place to look for information about past events and people. This time was no exception. The *Sentinel* noted, in 1924, that Gene Dick's house in Turkey Hill had burned to the ground. Funds were raised by townspeople to build a new home on a "road from Everett Howard's and the station," now called Howard Street. "Friends expect to erect this new building on Saturday and have it ready for occupancy at night." It was suggested that many would have dishes, furniture, etc., that they would be glad to donate to "warm up the house."

The article continued:

> *Magazines have their popular stories of people who render creditable accounts of themselves in spite of handicaps. Such a story might be written of Gene Dick, who in spite of the fact that he is almost totally blind, cares for himself, goes about unassisted, works every day on the ditch where he can usually locate his section, goes trapping and fishing, and refuses to be side tracked in life.*

The ditch reference leads to another story. In 1924 the Belchertown Water District had been formed and pipes were being laid to connect with the homes. Gene Dick had been hired by Water Commissioner Harold Ketchen to help dig the ditches. The late Gould Ketchen told me that his father recalled that Gene Dick was one of the best. All they had to do was lay out the ditch by placing two lines of string. He would use the string as his guide and the ditch was dug straight and true.

Summer

William Bridgman remembered another story about digging ditches, when he responded to the "Steeple" article on the death of Gene Dick. "I remember him too as a co-worker with pick and shovel digging foundations for the Belchertown State School, very early in the twenties. Given a line to follow, Gene threw out more earth—and rocks included—than any of the rest of us."

In 1932 the town closed the dump on Mill Valley Road because it was becoming a nuisance. They opened up a new dump on what they called the "Giguere dumping ground on the cross road between Maple Street and John W. Jackson Street." Now called Howard Street, it must have been near the home of Gene Dick. In 1933 several letters from Gene Dick, headlined "Wants Your Junk," appeared in the *Sentinel*. The letters stated that he was now taking care of the dump for the town. The letter had a long list of items that could be left at the dump or at his house. The list included rags, clothes, beds, mattresses and bed clothes, blankets, carpets, grain bags, all kinds of metal—big or small—batteries, magazines, automobile tires and rubber tubes, cook stoves, etc. He signed off "Neighbor to all, I thank you and Good-bye." It sounded as if we had a one stop "recycling center" right in the center of town.

Charles Howard, who still lives on Jackson Street, remembers Gene Dick:

> *I remember him very well, as I saw him often. Every time I went to the dump, he was there poking over the trash looking for metals, which he sold. He carried a magnet to help distinguish iron and steel from other metals. He trapped animals in the cold weather, especially skunks and skinned them and sold the fur. He always smelled like a skunk as he must have been their target many times. His water came from a delightful spring across the road from his house where he hung a dipper to drink from and to fill his pails.*

Warren Barrett of Maple Street remembers him as an old man who traveled all over town with a walking stick. He walked up and down the hill to his little one-room house that was in back of the Barrett residence on Howard Street. Warren's grandfather, Herbert Harry Barrett, owned a cider and sawmill on Howard Street. It was a busy place during cider season. Another old man, Fred Nooney, helped out in the mill and had a room there. He and Gene Dick spent a lot of time together. Gene Dick would buy cider at five cents a gallon. "He might have stored up the cider—which would eventually turn hard—to keep himself warm in the winter."

Gene had many friends and neighbors. They certainly must have helped him in time of need. But he was self-sufficient in many ways. He was noted for his gardening, with hardly a weed in sight, and he raised chickens to make a modest living.

Trying to put together a story with bits and pieces of history is seldom satisfactory. There are always questions. That is certainly the case with the story of Gene Dick. What were his early years like? Town records show that his parents had three sons. Census records from 1880 show a Eugene Dixon, age seven, living at the Town

Farm. Pelham town records list a marriage of Eugene Dixon, twenty-seven, of Belchertown and Mabel Nutting, eighteen, of Pelham on November 17, 1900.

In 1940 the town closed the dump on Howard Street and reopened the dump on Mill Valley Road, so Gene Dick was no longer the "keeper of the dump." His obituary said he lived alone until about ten years before his death. When did he leave Howard Street? He is said to have been living with a family on Federal Street during the late 1950s before going to South Hadley in 1963.

The story isn't finished. These are only a few of the stories and facts that I have gleaned over the past several months. I have yet to find a picture of Gene Dick. I know there are a few more tales that would add to the history about Eugene Dixon, a true rugged individualist.

Doris Dickinson

"Old Home Week," 1902

The seeds of the formation of a historical society for Belchertown were planted during that great "Old Home Week" celebration held in Belchertown during the weekend of July 27, 1902. The Massachusetts Legislature in that year passed an act authorizing cities and towns of the Commonwealth to appropriate money for the purpose of an Old Home Week gathering, designating that weekend for the homecoming of the sons and daughters of the state.

The town appropriated one hundred dollars for the necessary expenses. An Old Home Week Association was formed. Invitations were mailed to six hundred former residents all over the United States. The invitation read: "All the sons and daughters of Belchertown, either by birth, descent or adoption, are cordially invited to join with the residents of the town in celebration of Old Home Week, beginning July 27, 1902."

Records of that old association have been lost, but remnants of that occasion remain in the archives of the Stone House Museum. They include invitations, lists and addresses of those invited, programs and newspaper articles. Most important of all is a book that was printed after the event. This book contains a list of the officers of the association, committee members, a description of all the events, speeches given by former pastors, citizens and descendants of early settlers. The newspaper account gave long lists of people who returned to Belchertown from all over the state, Connecticut, Rhode Island, New York, Ohio and Illinois. Dwight P. Clapp of New York and Belchertown was chairman of the Reception Committee.

It was a busy weekend. An "illumination" on Saturday evening began with a bonfire at the south end of the Common. Nearly all of the houses and stores in the village were illuminated and many of the houses "were handsomely decorated with flags and bunting."

Union services in the Congregational church on Sunday morning were followed by a service of song in the Baptist church in the evening. The high school alumni were in charge of the speeches given on Monday afternoon in the Methodist church. That evening there was music and a historical presentation by Lucy Thomson. At the Congregational church on Tuesday afternoon, the main speaker was Archibald Howe of Cambridge, Massachusetts. A descendant of Dr. Estes Howe, Belchertown's first doctor and a surgeon in the Revolutionary War, he told of the life of his ancestor. The celebration ended that evening with a reception in the town hall—that's the Old Town Hall on Park Street—with over five hundred in attendance.

One newspaper account stated, "No other feature of the Old Home Week entertainment was quite equal to the exhibit of arts and crafts and the loan collection, which filled the three rooms at the Congregational Chapel. It was a great surprise to the people of the town, who were not aware of the possibilities of this exhibition."

The exhibit was arranged by Mrs. George Thomson and her daughter, Lucy Thomson, in an effort to illustrate the history of the town. There were articles representing the history and life of the town since its settlement in 1731; old papers throwing light upon its early days; the journal of Justus Dwight, born here in 1739; Captain Nathaniel Dwight's account of the Crown Point expedition in 1755; Lieutenant James Walker's Revolutionary journal from 1778: old letters, tax bills, newspapers and currency; powder horns dating from the French and Indian War; Revolution-era canteens, swords, cartridge belts and drums; furniture used by the early settlers; old portraits; the hat worn by Elijah Coleman Bridgman in China; and articles of everyday use. The handiwork of the women of those early days was well represented with quilts, woven counterpanes and clothing, including early wedding dresses. There was a rare old pocketbook, jewelry, skeins of raw silk made from cocoons when the mulberry industry flourished here, a collection of Indian relics found in Belchertown, an ancient piano and a pitch pipe.

"Contrasting with the handiwork of the past was the exhibit of the crafts of today, which surprised many by its variety and excellence, though it was far from being a complete representation of the work now done in town," the newspaper stated. Lucy Thomson, who had started the Belchertown Arts and Crafts Society, exhibited a half dozen different patterns of the "Subbekashe rug," the "hooked" rug of new, all wool material that was being designed, colored and made in town. The Moore Moss Company displayed a life-size representation of a scene from Little Red Riding Hood and had other small articles of moss work manufactured by the company. Fred Purdy had a large collection of his Belchertown photographs and Mr. Squires displayed his large splint baskets.

> # Belchertown, Massachusetts.
>
> ## Old Home Week.
>
> All the sons and daughters of Belchertown, either by birth, descent or adoption, are cordially invited to join with the residents of the town in the celebration of Old Home Week, beginning July 27, 1902.
>
> ### Old Home Week Association.

Above and opposite: Two pages from the program from Old Home Week, 1902.

This list just scratches the surface of the articles that filled the three rooms in the chapel. As the newspaper stated, "the numerous articles worthy of mention would occupy more space than has already been given this article." This exhibition planted the seed that came to fruition the following year when a group of citizens met at the home of Dr. George Thomson on March 7, 1903, to form the Belchertown Historical Association. People saw the wealth of historical materials available in Belchertown that needed to be preserved for future generations. The Belchertown Historical Association collection started with many of the same artifacts that were displayed at the exhibition. They still remain in the Stone House Museum. For one hundred years, the association has collected and preserved materials that reflect the history and the people of Belchertown from the early 1700s to the present day.

Doris Dickinson

Programme.

Saturday Evening, July 26.

Illumination.

Sunday, July 27.

Union Services.
10.45 A. M. in Congregational Church.
7.30 P. M. Service of Song in Baptist Church.

Monday, July 28.

Exercises in charge of High School Alumni.
4 P. M. Speaking in M. E. Church.

Monday, 8 P. M.

Evening of Music, with Historical Paper.

Tuesday, July 29.

2 P. M. Exercises in Congregational Church.
Address of Welcome.
Responses by Distinguished Guests
and Prominent Citizens of the Town.

Tuesday Evening.

Reception in Town Hall from 8 to 10 P. M.

A House That Was a Home

As I drive past the new housing development on North Main Street in Belchertown, I am reminded of William and Marion Shaw, whose house was torn down to make way for this new project.

Seeing the old house torn down last fall saddened me, because it seemed to hold within its walls the echoes of the good times I had there. At the time of the demolition of the house, we had been further saddened by the death of Marion Hackett, daughter of the Shaws, who was brought up in that house. It was, to me, an eerie and poignant coincidence that the death of the house and one of its former occupants occurred within days of each other.

William Shaw served as town treasurer, tax collector and clerk for many years. His last job before his retirement was as the first manager of the Belchertown branch of the Ludlow Savings Bank. He was a man whose integrity was never questioned, a leader in his church and a pillar of the community. William died in 1968 and Marion died in 1965.

The Shaws had two daughters, Marion and Marjorie. Marion, whose death I noted earlier, was a missionary with her husband for many years in Burma. Much more could be said of her fine work in her profession, not the least of which was to translate the Bible into the Burmese language. Marjorie was killed in an automobile accident in 1969. She was a charming and beautiful woman, whose death had a profound affect on all that knew her.

Of these people who lived in the North Main Street home, the elder Marion Shaw had the greatest influence on my life, for Marion was my fifth- and sixth-grade teacher. She was the only teacher that motivated me to reach my potential. I attained the top honor roll for the two years that I was in her classes. Never again would my name appear on a school honor roll!

Marion would start the day by reading a part of a book, such as *The Secret Garden* or *The Boy Captive of Old Deerfield*. The former book is a classic in English literature and a departure from the previous "Dick and Jane" types of stories we had heard. When the latter book was finished, the class would be taken to Old Deerfield, where we could relive the attack of the French and Indians on the town. Our ten-year-old imaginations were in high gear as we viewed the battered door of one of the settlers' homes that the Indians tried to chop through with their tomahawks. We saw Bloody Brook and could imagine how it got its name. The trip to Deerfield was one of the examples of how Marion Shaw taught. She also was a fine pianist and would accompany us at our music lessons. Marion had the ability to motivate her students to do their very best.

The good times in the Shaw home included helping Marion make her famous peanut butter fudge or rehearsing for a play or skit for school or church. Her interest

Marion Shaw and one of her many classes at Center School.

in her pupils did not end in the schoolyard. Those of us who went to our church suppers remember her great Waldorf salads. I always made sure I was seated near the salad, for it was gobbled up in a short time.

The Shaws had four grandchildren, William and Martha Hackett, and David and Richard Powell. William is a professional opera singer in Austria. Martha is a clinical nurse in Boston's Chinatown. David lives in northern Vermont and owns a chain of appliance stores. Richard is a physician and resides in Florida. Surely, the talents and values of William and Marion Shaw, enhanced by their daughters, have been successfully passed on to their grandchildren and no doubt will transfer to their great-grandchildren.

Now another old house has been demolished. I wonder what are the thoughts of those occupants still living, as they look at the empty lot.

Harvey Dickinson

Home Again

More than 2,000 people in the Swift River Valley were forced from their homes to provide water for the city of Boston and its environs. This evacuation went on from late 1920 to 1938, as the homes were purchased by the state. Some were sold for scrap, burned or taken apart and rebuilt somewhere else. More than 6,500 bodies were dug up and reburied somewhere else. It was as if the authorities were trying to erase any trace of places where people were born, lived and died. The one thing that could not be erased was the memories of those who lived there.

It has been said, "You can't go home again," but for me, the nearest thing to going home was to see my grandparents' house again after nearly eighty years.

A small book called *Quabbin to Dorset* was brought to my attention that showed houses in their Quabbin Valley locations and then in Dorset, Vermont. My grandparents' Prescott home was one of those dismantled and rebuilt in Dorset. I was not aware that the house had been moved to Dorset until just a short time ago.

Why were all those homes moved so far from Quabbin—and in the depths of the Great Depression of the 1930s? A man from Dorset that owned a trucking company wanted to keep his drivers on the payroll. He was able to buy these homes for next to nothing. He dismantled and hauled them to Dorset where they were rebuilt and sold to some of the moneyed people in town. Not all were kept in the original design, but they were done well in a different manner.

When I told my nieces about this, we all decided to go to Dorset and find their great-grandparents' and my grandparents' old home. The photo of the home in the Dorset setting showed dormers had been added, but it was otherwise recognizable. We toured around the town looking for the home, but could not find the place shown in the book's photo. The logical place to start our research was the historical society, but we found it closed. The library provided us with the phone number of the gentlemen who wrote the book. We called him and he was happy to tell us how to get to the house. He told us the road to take and to look for a driveway marked by a pair of stone piers. We could not see the house from that point and a sign informed us that this was a private road. After driving for three hours to get to Dorset, we were not going to be deterred from our goal. We drove up the long winding gravel road and found the house. From the rear view, we did not recognize it as my grandparents'. There was a car in the yard, which meant someone was at home. A young man came out of the house and headed down the drive and stopped to find out who we were. He lived in Dorset in his own home, and this place had just been bought by folks from New Jersey as a summer residence. He gave us his name and phone number, telling us to stay and look around.

The home of Julia Thresher in Prescott prior to being moved for the construction of the Quabbin Reservoir.

We then went around to the front—and there was the house, facing a magnificent view of the Vermont mountains! There it was, my grandparents' home forming the center of an expanded mansion (yes, a mansion). What a gorgeous place it was! Among the additions was a front porch with a marble floor. Beside the house was a guest cottage, completing the concept of a great summer place.

It was a good and warm feeling, being there, knowing that the old house on Prescott Hill that I had visited as a child eighty years ago still exists in such a glorious setting. I am fortunate in a way—I can still go home again.

Harvey Dickinson

Autumn

BELCHERTOWN'S HIGH SCHOOLS

How many high schools has Belchertown built over the years? Recently, while reorganizing some photographs in the archives at the Stone House, I wrote on the envelope "old high school." That school was Lawrence Memorial Hall. That got me to thinking. I couldn't just write "old high school" because there were other buildings that could bear that same designation.

Making sure that the right names and information are on pictures is important for future researchers. Too many times I have gone to auctions, antique shops or even tag sales and found boxes of old photographs with no names. I am sad when I look at them, for I see lost history. But wait—I was writing about high schools.

A high school building, built by private subscription of twenty-seven proprietors for $100 a share, was started in 1829. It was built on land owned by Dr. Estes Howe at the north end of the Common. There was a difference of opinion among the proprietors and the building stood unfinished for six years and was used, for a time, as a carriage shop by H.T. Filer. Eventually, the proprietors relinquished their interest and a group of "public spirited men" finished the building and sold it to a Reverend Mr. Foote for $1,800. It was called the Belchertown Classical School and had tuition students from surrounding towns and even as far away as Louisiana. It flourished for a while, but had its ups and downs. At the annual town meeting in March 1846, Adolphus Strong, one of those "public spirited men" who finished the school, offered to continue the school if the town would allow him $200 a year, taking it from the fund appropriated by the town for schools. But the article was passed over. Mr. Strong was obliged, for want of means, to discontinue the school. The building became the Belcher House, a renowned summer hotel. Later, it became the Park View Hotel, which burned in May of 1928.

The School Committee Report for the year 1864–65 stated:

> *We desire to call attention to one other topic. By a law of this Commonwealth which is in substance almost as old as the State itself, each town of five hundred*

families is required to maintain a high school for ten months at least each year. In the twenty-eighth Annual Report of the Board of Education, just published, we are informed that there are sixty-eight towns in the state which are required to support such a school. One of these is Belchertown. We are also informed that thirty-two of these towns failed to comply with the requisition of this Statute; that one of these towns is located in Hampshire County and that one is Belchertown. We confess, for ourselves, that we are not fond of this kind of notoriety.

These words must have prompted some action, for the report of the Board of Selectmen for the year ending February 15, 1868, reported that Belchertown had spent $4,520.39 to build a new high school and that included "furnishings." The report listed every amount spent and the workmen involved, including an amount for four dollars to a Mrs. Wiley for scrubbing the floors. Belchertown had built its first high school in 1867, opening late in the fall of that year. The first class graduated in 1869. It was a two-story wooden building on what is now the site of Center School, off Maple Street. While built as a high school, additions were made through the years for grammar and intermediate classrooms. It stood for fifty-four years, but burned in November of 1921, leaving no schools in the center of town. Just a year before, the town had appointed a committee to take preliminary steps to study the crowded school conditions in the center.

The old Belchertown High School was located in the center of town, where the school administration building is located today.

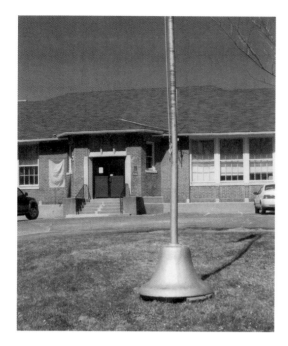

The old bell in front of the
school administration building.

Around the same time, the town was about to receive a bequest from Sara
Lawrence Robinson, wife of the former governor of Kansas, Dr. Charles Robinson,
and daughter of Myron Lawrence of Belchertown. In her will, she had left a bequest
of $40,000 to build a hall in honor of her father. She had already purchased the
site of the old Highland Hotel in the center of town. After much deliberation, the
trustees of the Robinson trust, the selectman and the committee appointed to build
a new high school went to the probate court and the attorney general to draw up a
contract that would allow the addition of schoolrooms on the rear of the hall. The
town would accept the hall and provide for the maintenance.

The town held a special town meeting for authorization of its first bond issue for school
construction of $50,000—$30,000 for the high school and $20,000 for a Center Grade
School. The town approved the contract and the combined Lawrence Memorial Hall
and high school was built for a total of $64,500. The high school opened in September
of 1923. Center School, built on the site of the old high school, opened in December
of 1922. Built eighty-two years ago, Center School might be our oldest school building
in continuous use. It is now the offices of the superintendent of schools.

A relic of that old high school building still remains—people drive by it everyday
not knowing. The school committee report for the next year had this to say, "A steel
flag pole has been erected at the Grade school, using the bell from the old building
as a support, thus perpetuating forever the memories connected with the former
structure and serving to link the old with the new."

Autumn

Within a short two-year span, the town built two new schools and a new town hall. The town hall housed offices for the town clerk and the board of selectmen. The hall and the stage were used by the high school. Little noticed portraits commissioned by Sara Lawrence Robinson—of herself, Governor Robinson, Myron Lawrence, her sister and her nephew—hang on the walls of Lawrence Memorial Hall. Interestingly enough, an earlier portrait of her mother, Clarissa Dwight Lawrence, hangs in the dining room of the Stone House Museum.

The building served as a high school for forty-two years until, once again, crowded school conditions prompted the formation of another school building committee. Groundbreaking for a Belchertown Junior-Senior High School was held in July of 1963 on North Washington Street. It was dedicated in May of 1965 and was built at a cost of $1.2 million. Donald Geer, then a resident of Belchertown and a graduate of Belchertown High School, was appointed principal. This school, after thirty-seven years, was closed in 2002 with the opening of the present Belchertown High School on Old Springfield Road. The closed school has reopened, after renovations, as the Jabish Brook Middle School. Construction on the current high school started on April 26, 2000, and the building was occupied in September 2002. The cost of the new building—$32.5 million dollars.

This brief article just skims the surface of the histories of most of these buildings, each going through almost the same process—growing school populations forcing the town to assess school needs, committees recommending new buildings, building committees appointed and special town meetings held to approve plans, sites and costs—none without some controversy—but the town ultimately voting to provide, to the best of their ability, suitable educational facilities for the education of the children of Belchertown.

So, if my research is correct, it would seem that Belchertown has erected four high school buildings over the past 134 years. After the high school was built in 1867, the school committee in their annual report had this to say:

The great event in the history of education in this town the past year has been the building of a house for a high school, the establishment of the school and its successful progress for two terms. We see in it the promise of a great blessing to the town. With a course of study, already marked out, equal to that in our first class academies, it sets before all the children of the town privileges to be reached by them such as they have never seen before. Many of them already see in it the possibilities of a better life. By the stimulus it gives, they are lifted above influences that have led to the ruin of so many.

Perhaps similar words were echoed in the report of the School Committee after the present Belchertown High School opened.

Doris Dickinson

OTTO REIMANN, BOOKBINDER

T here are three words in the title of this article, but those three words tell a unique bit of history about a man, his passion and a little-known early industry in Belchertown.

Otto Reimann was born in Leipzig, Germany in 1867. He learned his trade in his native city and pursued it in many places, immigrating to New York in 1896. From New York he went to Charlotte, North Carolina, where he was foreman of the Queen City Bindery. It was there that he met and married Miss Bertha Dilger in 1907. They came to Belchertown about 1917, and purchased a farm on Allen Street where he opened his bookbindery.

Lewis Blackmer, editor of the *Belchertown Sentinel*, in a series of articles in 1922 about the industries of Belchertown, wrote about the bookbindery.

> *It is not located on our main street nor is it on the main arteries of travel, but the fact that people of discrimination seek it out among the hills of the northern section of our town is proof sufficient that it is worth talking about when we find it. If a man can bind a better book than his neighbor, as with the case of the mouse trap, the world beats a track to his door, no matter where he lives.*

Amherst College was evidently one institution that found their way to Mr. Reimann's door early. In 1921 the following small article appeared in the *Sentinel*:

> *Amherst College has just sent to Jeffrey John Archer Amherst, Viscount Holmesdale of Montreal, Seven Oaks, Kent, England, a beautiful souvenir volume commemorative of the centennial celebration at commencement. The Springfield Union says this regarding it: "The book was bound by Otto Reimann of North Belchertown, an expert craftsman, who used brown morocco and hand tooled designs in gold leaf inlaid with red and hand lettered throughout to produce this gem of bookbinder's art." Mr. Reimann does a large amount of regular work for the colleges at Amherst.*

He also executed for Amherst College a commission for books sent to England for the centennial. Perhaps one of his most memorable works can still be viewed at Forbes Library in Northampton in their special collections. In 1924 he was commissioned to bind a set of thirty-five books, known as the President Coolidge Collection. The books were bound with blue imported English linen with a gold star inlaid in each corner to correspond with the Coolidge flag. Seven of the books were large volumes and the rest were small. One of the smaller ones was an especially poignant book and was entitled *Tribute to Calvin Coolidge Jr.* The book

Otto Riemann, bookbinder.

contained the sermon delivered at the funeral of the president's son. It was one of the first volumes to be completed and was a gift to the Coolidge family.

While Mr. Reimann bound books for what was then the Massachusetts Agricultural College, Amherst College, Forbes Library, Jones Library and many of the faculty of these colleges, he still had time for local needs. He bound Town Reports for the Belchertown Historical Association. A bill in the archives, dated January 28, 1926, shows that he bound five volumes of town reports at $1.80 each, for a total of $9.00. He also did work for Clapp Memorial Library, including the binding of the *Sentinel* from the publication of the first number.

Mr. Reimann came to Belchertown for his health, but continued to ply his trade and passion, sometimes making special tools for his work. He died on May 4, 1927, and is buried in Mount Hope Cemetery in Belchertown.

In his obituary, Mr. Blackmer said, "During his residence here, Mr. Reimann seldom came to town and few people realized the extent of his contribution. He counted among his best friends professors at Amherst College and Jones Library, officials for whom he did a large amount of work and who often visited him at his shop in his country home, and remembered him in his days of incapacity." Some of those professors and officials were his pallbearers.

In 1930 Jones Library mounted an exhibit of his work. The *Springfield Union* had this to say about the exhibit:

> *It is well occasionally to revive the memory of men and women who do things. And one of the favorite and most effective ways of doing this is through exhibits of their work. The Jones Library, this week has on view an exhibit of the work of one of the most interesting characters ever to come into the immediate section, Otto Reimann, bookbinder and master craftsman in his art. He moved to Belchertown in 1917 and for 10 years plied his trade, with ill health staring him in the face, but never losing sight of the fact that intrinsic beauty lay at his finger tips. Mass production has crowded out of circulation so many of the handmade arts and the world has lost, in its craze for speed and efficiency, much of the beauty and fine detail that characterized the hand-wrought piece. Otto Reimann never turned out a piece that was not worthy of his reputation. Meticulous, careful, of a charming personality. All of these attributes were reflected in his work.*

At the closing of his article on industries in Belchertown, Mr. Blackmer wrote,

> *Like the true artist, he does not pretend really to have learned his trade, but is all the time reaching out into undiscovered possibilities that make his work more worthwhile. No write-up like this is necessary to bolster up Mr. Reimann's business. He already is 'sold' weeks ahead. Our main purpose in calling this industry to the attention of our readers is to drive home the truth that in good old Belchertown there can be and is being produced something that the world wants.*

Doris Dickinson

Opposite: The building on Jabish Street that once housed Belchertown Motor Sales is now occupied by a laundromat.

CARRIAGES TO CARS

F our want ads and an advertisement in an early *Sentinel* sparked my interest recently and started me on another research adventure into Belchertown history. The ads heralded a change that marked the beginning of what would forever alter the look of Belchertown streets.

In the October 21, 1921 issue, there appeared three ads offering horses for sale and another advertising stalls for rent in a barn. In the same issue was an ad for a one-ton truck being sold by the Ford Agency owned by D.D. Hazen, "Authorized Agent." Daniel Dwight Hazen, who owned Hazen's Store for many years, had recently sold the business. He had constructed a new building at the beginning of Jabish Street, now housing a laundromat, and opened the "first Ford Agency in Belchertown." Mr. Hazen is said to have met Henry Ford on several of Ford's visits to Belchertown with Gaston Plantiff. Mr. Plantiff, a Belchertown native, was the first northeast regional sales manager of the Ford Motor Company.

Corn fodder and one horse in "good, sound condition" were being offered by Hager Brothers of Belchertown. The Gulf Refining Company of Palmer had four horses for sale, one pair of bays and one pair of grays with harnesses, claiming they were "disposing of horses because we are displacing them with auto trucks." Someone on North Main and Walnut Streets was looking to rent two stalls in their barn "or can be used for auto storage."

Harold B. Ketchen's ad stated "FOR SALE—1 good, general purpose horse. One harness with collar and hames, 1 light carry-all as good as new. An ideal outfit for school children." This ad was particularly interesting because Mr. Ketchen owned a Dodge Agency in town. In fact, the 1917 *Sentinel* had an ad for the Belchertown Garage: "H.B. Ketchen, Prop., Agent for Dodge Cars—Cars for Rent." Maybe he had taken the "outfit" in trade. He was also the proprietor of the Belchertown-Granby-Holyoke bus line, but that is another story.

The Model T Ford Agency became Belchertown Motor Sales in 1924, when Frank L. Gold joined the firm. In 1926, it became a Chevrolet Agency and, in 1940, a Hudson/Nash Agency. Mr. Gold operated a garage with the agency until 1958, when he sold the building.

In 1921 the days of the horse and buggy along the tree-lined dirt roads of Belchertown were fast disappearing. The horse sheds alongside the Congregational church, where parishioners left their carriages during services, would disappear. The Curtis blacksmith shop on South Main Street, one of the last in Belchertown, would close its doors in 1938 after almost a century of doing business.

Belchertown, called the "Detroit of the carriage industry" by later historians, would no longer see the carriages that once made it famous. Remnants remain housed in the building known as the Ford Annex on the grounds of the Stone House Museum. Ironically, the man who brought about the demise of the horse and buggy era gave money to the Belchertown Historical Association to preserve the carriages and sleighs once made in Belchertown.

Doris Dickinson

HENRY FORD

With antique cars on the Stone House lawn and antique carriages in the Ford Annex, the history of transportation comes together in an interesting way. Belchertown, once called the "Detroit of the carriage industry," had connections to Henry Ford through Belchertown native Gaston Plantiff.

The *Belchertown Sentinel*, during its first year of publication, ran this short news item on October 8, 1915: "Gaston Plantiff, a son of Belchertown, and Henry Ford, the automobile King, had the pleasure of dining with President Wilson at Washington recently. Mr. Plantiff has charge of the New York branch and assembly plant of the Ford Motor Co. Recent additions to this plant make it one of the largest commercial buildings in the city."

In December, another article appeared:

Gaston Plantiff of New York sailed on Saturday for Europe with Henry Ford and his company of Peace promoters gathered from far and near, on a specially chartered ship. Mr. Plantiff is the manager of the New York branch of the Ford Motor Co. and is the first salesman Mr. Ford ever employed. Belchertown people who remember him as a newsboy are glad to see him in a position of prominence. His mother and sister, Mrs. Ida King, have gone to New York to see him before he sails.

Henry Ford.

The *Belchertown Sentinel*, on October 19, 1917, announced that D.D. Hazen, agent for the Ford Motor Company, was purchasing a site at the beginning of Jabish Street and would erect a Ford Demonstration Building. "The building is to be of brick and will be quite citified in appearance." The article went on to say that the plans had been drawn by an architect and had been approved by the Ford Motor Company, although the enterprise was a personal one. "Mr. Hazen now has the Ford agency in a good share of the following five towns: Belchertown, Granby, Enfield, Greenwich and Prescott."

When Mr. Ford visited Belchertown with Gaston Plantiff in the early 1920s, Mr. Hazen had been in business for over five years. It is said that he not only sold the cars, but also taught people how to drive them. The building is still standing next to Lawrence Memorial Hall and is now known as the Jabish Street Laundromat.

Later on, Henry Ford came to Belchertown several times when Gaston came to visit his mother and sister. One of these times was during 1922 when the Trustees of the Belchertown Historical Association were opening the Stone House for use as a museum. Mr. Plantiff brought Mr. Ford to visit the site. A barn at the rear of the property was in poor condition and the trustees were debating whether to repair or remove the structure. They already had some carriages for the barn. He must have played on Ford's generosity and several months later the Association received a check for $5,000. The Ford Annex was built of native fieldstone out of the fields and stone walls around the area. Daniel P. Spencer and his son, Howard, were the local stonemasons. Gaston Plantiff represented Mr. Ford at the dedication of the annex.

The last time Mr. Ford came to Belchertown was for the funeral service for Gaston Plantiff in 1934. Mr. Plantiff is buried in Mount Hope cemetery.

Doris Dickinson

EVERETT CLAPP HOUSE

The Everett Clapp home at 26 South Main Street, now owned by Christine Shirtcliff, was built in 1810 and extensively remodeled in 1883 in the Queen Anne style by New York architect Henry Kilburn who was the architect for Clapp Memorial Library. A house is more than its architectural details, however. When it was built and the builder are important, but what really makes the history of a house are the people who lived there over the years.

In 1812 Mark Doolittle came to Belchertown to practice law and purchased the house from William Holland, the first owner. It was a large square house with a hipped tin roof with an ell running west and no porches. The James Clapp homestead next to it was similar.

Mark Doolittle, a graduate of Yale and Middlebury Colleges, practiced law in Belchertown for over forty years. He was a prolific writer and popular as a speaker. He served as a state representative and Senator, was on the governor's council and was a county commissioner for many years. Early historical accounts said his home was quite a social center. He is probably best remembered as the author of *A Historical Sketch of the Congregational Church in Belchertown* published in 1852. The book contains a history of the town, a listing of all the members of the church from its beginning until 1850, and genealogies of some of the early settlers. A quote from Doolittle's obituary had these words: "It is from local histories that all histories are made."

The house at 26 South Main Street, known as the Everett Clapp House, is now the Shirtcliff residence.

In the early 1880s, Everett Clapp bought the house and moved it back from the street. It was renovated in the Queen Anne style, although not as elaborate as the Dwight Clapp house next door. It is said that some remnants of that first old house can still be seen within the present structure. It still retains, on the right side of the house, one of the porte-cocheres used for sheltering people entering or leaving carriages. The ell on the back of the old house became the cottage that still stands on the property. A barn or carriage house was erected that was similar to the Dwight Clapp barn, but was removed several years ago. At the time of the renovations, one of the old mantels from the Doolittle home was installed in the Dr. George Thomson home at 22 South Main Street. Dr. Thomson's mother was Lucy Doolittle, daughter of Mark Doolittle.

Everett Clapp and his wife, Romelia, and their son, Knight, used the home as a summer residence for a number of years. Everett served as the first president of the board of trustees of the Clapp Memorial Library and, along with his brother Dwight, supervised the building of Clapp Memorial Library. He sold the home in 1901 to Letitia M. Warner. Through the years other families have lived in this old home. Names that still are remembered by some: Bardwell, Witt, Stewart, Calabrese, Engle, Bucholz. Each added to the history of the house and made changes just as Everett Clapp did.

Doris Dickinson

Bardwell's Votometer

The election is over, the votes have been counted and the winners have been declared. The electronic voting machines used at the Belchertown polls quickly gave their counts. What most voters and the workers at the polls did not know was that one of the first mechanical voting machines was designed and patented by a Belchertown native.

Richard Garvey, area historian and former editor of the *Springfield Union*, recently devoted two columns to this first voting machine. "Votometer Blazed the Trail" was the headline of one column. The machine was the brainchild of Arthur Bardwell, whose ancestors were among the first settlers of Cold Spring. Garvey went on to say that the nation's first voting machines were made in Springfield almost a century ago—the mechanisms in a shop on Main Street and the woodwork on State Street. They were first used in Northampton, Massachusetts, in 1900.

Arthur Bardwell was born in that part of south Belchertown once known as "Bardwell Village" and later known as "Skeeterville." There was even a railroad stop at the village known as Bardwell Station. It is said that he attended Franklin School in his early years. His father, Frank Bardwell, conducted an extensive business manufacturing woolen cloth. After the mill burned, the family moved to Springfield in 1876, where his father bought and operated a farm. Arthur was sent to Wilbraham Academy, then to Harvard and finally to Cornell, where he received his degree in civil engineering.

An artist's sketch of Bardwell's Votometer.

A photograph from the Northampton special election in which the Votometer was first demonstrated.

The City of Northampton bought the first seven Votometers for only one dollar each, so the company could conduct an official test. It was used during their special election on August 28, 1899. The *Northampton Daily Herald* on August 29 headlined "Voting Machines a Decided Success." The article went on to say, "The polls in the special city election yesterday closed at 4 o'clock and at exactly 4:03 the returns from ward one were placed in the hands of City Clerk Clapp and within another four minutes the returns from every ward in the city had been received and announced. The Bardwell Votometer Co. certainly scored a decisive victory for its machine yesterday, by the ease with which the vote was handled." A company publication described the machine as one that allowed a more accurate method of voting, prevented fraud, maintained secrecy and made it possible to get returns promptly. Several states sent officials to Northampton to observe the voting and the use of the machines.

Garvey went on to say in his article that the success in Northampton attracted the attention of the Franklin Institute, which recommended that the city of Philadelphia confer its John Scott Medal on Bardwell, and that honor was presented in 1901.

Unfortunately, Bardwell saw his company get into political and financial difficulties and the company went bankrupt before the machines could be widely used. Northampton had acquired five more machines and planned to use them, but decided to wait because the company was in bankruptcy. They waited in vain and in 1904 voted to return to paper ballots.

There is much more to tell about the machine and its history, but to bring it to an end, we note that Arthur Bardwell later returned to his native town, became active in town affairs, particularly in securing a water supply for the town, and died at his home on South Main Street on March 15, 1945. There is no known Votometer in existence. Several years ago, I asked Mr. Garvey if he knew what happened to the machines in Northampton. He believes they were broken up for scrap. Harvey Dickinson, who lived next door to the Bardwells, remembered Mr. Bardwell. He remembered "a fine gentleman" sitting in his room surrounded by books and papers. But even more incredible, he remembered seeing a Bardwell Votometer. It was housed in the small house at the rear of the property. Nothing is known about what happened to this machine, perhaps the last Votometer. So went a part of Belchertown and Northampton history.

But bits and pieces of this interesting footnote to history still remain. The Stone House Museum preserves part of that history. The John Scott Medal, awarded to Bardwell by the city of Philadelphia, still resides in its impressive case, along with patent documents with their colorful ribbons and stamps from the United States and Canada, the report on the Votometer by the New York State Commission on Voting Machines, and company brochures. How wonderful it would be to find, tucked away in some dusty town hall basement in New York or New Jersey, a Bardwell Votometer!

Doris Dickinson

GEEZER SHOES

A few weeks ago, I stopped to say hello to my friend Dave at his work. He greeted me with, "I see you have on a new pair of geezer shoes."

"When did you become a fashion expert?" I asked. "You, a man from Cooleyville, who didn't own a necktie until a few years ago." When the occasion called for a necktie, he had to borrow one from his neighbors.

I asked him how he learned of the term "geezer shoes." He told me that a couple of years ago, he and his wife were going on a trip to the Caribbean and he had gone to Wal-Mart for some shoes for the occasion. When Dave proudly showed his wife, Suzie, his new shoes, she said, "If you wear those 'geezer shoes' on this trip, you will be going alone."

At this point, it became apparent that Dave was right. These shoes were geezer shoes, for I remembered that the only persons that I had ever seen wearing them were old and a lot of them were in nursing homes.

Geezer shoes.

These shoes are a sort of sneaker, either black or blue, with Velcro straps instead of laces. Velcro straps are for kids that don't know how to tie laces or for old people who forgot how. I will say this for them, they are very comfortable, cheap and made in China, as is nearly everything worn these days.

I don't wear these shoes in public anymore, for I'm not ready for "geezerhood" quite yet. My ninety-one-year-old brother-in-law, who hears, sees and thinks better than I, wears geezer shoes. Okay, if I get to ninety, I will wear my geezer shoes, but by that time, unlike my brother-in-law, I will be lucky to know if I am wearing anything.

Harvey Dickinson

PEAT BOGS

T hat cool Canadian air is filtering into Belchertown these days. Piles of cordwood are being stacked in dooryards, oil tanks are being filled and the stock market is quoting the cost of oil at over fifty dollars a barrel. "Residents warm up to alternative heating sources" was a recent newspaper headline.

When I came to Belchertown in the 1940s, I was introduced to the intricacies of the coal furnace. Clarence Robinson would arrive with a truck from Ryther and Warren Mill with a ton of coal. He would shovel the coal down a chute and into a coal bin in the basement. I learned how to keep the furnace going during the day and how to bank it for the night. How I wished, at times, for that "alternative heating source" I had in Oklahoma—natural gas. Just turn on the jet and strike a match!

An unusual alternative heating source was once considered in Belchertown. An article appeared in the July 24, 1866 issue of the *Hampshire Gazette and Northampton Courier*, datelined Belchertown. A joint-stock company had been formed with a capital of $20,000 for the purpose of "rendering new fuel." It seems that there were "immense beds of peat existing in the immediate vicinity of the railroad depot." The peat had been subjected to tests and proved to be of a "very superior" quality, and "as the company has control of some forty acres, from six to twelve feet deep and lying directly on the railroad and with a good chance for drainage, their facilities for furnishing the fuel promptly and cheaply at any point, are hard to beat." Some forty or so years later, another article appeared, from all indications in a Springfield paper, which gave additional information about this business venture. Evidently peat was once again being touted as an alternative fuel:

> *So much has been said and written recently in connection with the new fuel and the matter is receiving so much attention, especially in the vicinity of Boston, that some reminiscences connected with the peat industry which caused an important era in its manufacture and testing its qualities as a substitute for other kinds of fuel more than 40 years ago in Belchertown, may be of interest. It was sometime in the sixties that Dr. George F. Thomson returned from the Southern battlefields where he had been in service as a surgeon. Dr. Thomson, on his farm, owned a good number of acres of peat land. Associated in this business with Enoch Burnett, a considerable sum of money was put into this enterprise. At that time the manufacture of the peat was considered necessary, and quite expensive machinery was purchased to develop this industry. At that time the price of coal was $9 per ton and sometimes $10. The peat was made ready for fuel and samples of it were tested by the manufacturers of carriages in the shops and people in their homes, to*

the satisfaction of those who made the test. Those days there was not much fuel used except wood. The very general use of anthracite coal such as there now is was not thought of. But the price of coal soon became lower and the manufacture of peat was discontinued as there was not a sufficient call for it to warrant the continuance of its manufacture.

A look at the 1860 map of Belchertown shows that Dr. Thomson owned land from his house lot on South Main Street all the way down to the railroad tracks and beyond. Evidently in 1903, before the above article appeared, there had been a "coal famine" and peat was being suggested again as an alternative. The author of the article went on to say, "Should this industry receive much impetus, Belchertown has, according to the judgment of those best acquainted with its peat lands, more than 2,000 acres of peat bog, enough, it would seem for a substitute fuel in times such as last winter. The wood supply is each year growing less, the lumber, railroad ties and pulp mills call for large quantities of this product of the forests. But the peat bog remains intact."

In the February 15, 1918 issue of the *Sentinel*, an article was headlined "When Coal Was High." Once again, the story of the Belchertown venture and of the use of peat during times of fuel shortages or high prices was recounted. It quoted more current sources about the thousands of acres of peat bogs throughout New England.

The idea of two thousand acres of peat bogs in Belchertown piqued my interest. We've walked the road along the railroad tracks where this early peat manufacturing plant must have been located. Some of the bogs are still there, although some have been filled. I remember a bog on Federal Street just before the road to the town beach.

I contacted the conservation commission to see if there was a map that delineated peat bogs and was told the maps only designate wetlands. Since Belchertown has a lot of wetlands, there must be some of those acres of peat bogs still in existence. Little is heard these days of using peat in the United States, although large sections of the world still use this heating resource.

These newspaper articles give a glimpse of an early business venture, though short-lived, in Belchertown. I started this article telling about how I learned to run a coal furnace in our home on South Main Street. That furnace was located in the old home of Dr. George Thomson. I wonder if he tried out the peat in his furnace. Maybe it was used by the Cowles Carriage shops just down the street.

Doris Dickinson

TURKEYS

Over the past several years, we have seen flocks of turkeys in many sections of Belchertown, Amherst and New Salem. What a wonderful sight! Wild turkeys, like many other wild creatures, are becoming more and more noticeable in suburban settings.

A section of town is still called Turkey Hill. Tradition tells us this section owes its name to the fact that for years after the first settlers came, large numbers of turkeys, which then abounded in this region, gathered nightly from all points of the compass to roost in the heavy growth of timber which then covered this section. With the first appearance of dawn, the turkeys, separating into small flocks, would fly away to their usual feeding grounds, but the shades of evening would find them all back to their favorite roosting place. Native Americans enjoyed an abundant population of wild turkeys and hunted them for food. They created calls from turkey wing bones to help them bring turkeys close enough to kill. Benjamin Franklin called turkeys the "true American original." He wanted the turkey to be the national bird instead of the eagle. He admired their resourcefulness, agility, courage and beauty.

At the time of colonial settlement, the wild turkey was widespread in Massachusetts, ranging from Cape Cod to the Berkshires. As settlement progressed, however, hardwood forests were cut and the range of the turkey began to shrink. By the early 1800s turkeys were rare in the state, and the last-known native bird was killed on Mount Tom in 1851.

Between 1914 and 1947, Massachusetts Wildlife Federation tried four times to restore wild turkeys to Massachusetts. In 1960 Massachusetts Wildlife, in cooperation with the University of Massachusetts, tried again and introduced twenty-two turkeys in the Quabbin Reservation. While at first there was an initial surge in the population, it dropped quickly showing that game farm turkeys were not suitable for reestablishing a self-sustaining population. Wild turkeys were imported from New York and Pennsylvania and again introduced into Quabbin with the results more promising. Quabbin presented an ideal site for this experiment. It is about 98 percent forest, 15 percent of which was conifer plantations. Mown fields, pastures and other openings were adjacent in New Salem, just to the north.

The restoration of wild turkeys into Massachusetts has been successful, as evident of the flocks in the surrounding countryside. They have shown considerable adaptability to different habitat conditions. The restoration program has been so successful that now there is a hunting season for wild turkeys by permit. The fall season in Massachusetts starts on October 1 and runs to November 5. No turkey wing bone callers for these modern day hunters; the Internet is full of sites advertising equipment to catch this elusive bird. Just watch and see them disappear into the forest right before your eyes.

A view from one of Belchertown's turkey farms.

Even though the wild turkeys disappeared from Belchertown, in later years the raising of turkeys proved to be a lucrative business and provided local jobs. When Nelson Holland returned to the family farm on Old Enfield Road, which had been in his family since 1803, he purchased ten white turkeys in New York and brought them home to roost. From that small beginning emerged the raising of White Holland turkeys that were processed and shipped all over the eastern seaboard to grace Thanksgiving tables. The Anderson Turkey Farm on Turkey Hill Road was another site that flourished.

While both businesses are long gone, turkeys have returned to Belchertown, perhaps to be seen again on Turkey Hill.

Doris Dickinson

EDDIE PARENT, THE POPCORN MAN

Several weeks ago in the From Our Files column in the *Sentinel*, under the heading "Seventy Years Ago," Edward Parent announced that he was opening a hot popcorn stand in front of Clark's Barber Shop and that he was using Conkey's homegrown popcorn. If you were living in Belchertown seventy years ago, you might remember Eddie and his popcorn stand. You might even remember Charlie

Clark's barbershop with the pool table in the back. The barbershop was in the building where the pizza shop is located on Park Street. But just in case you aren't in that age category, this is a story about Edward Parent.

Eddie came to Belchertown about 1905. He was born in Ludlow on May 17, 1889, and for many years, he was a railroad section hand for the Central Vermont Railroad, working out of the local station. He enlisted in the army in October 1917, and was assigned to the Eleventh Railroad Engineers of the Twenty-sixth Division, arriving in France in December of that year. His regiment was with the English for nine months and saw action at Arras, Amiens, LaBassie and Cambrai. At Cambrai, he was so seriously wounded that he was unable to return to active service and spent many months in the hospital. He did, however, act as an interpreter for the Second Army Corps before returning to this country. He started working again for the railroad. He joined the American Legion and was a past commander of the Chauncey D. Walker Post and was also a member of the Hampshire County Voiture, "40 and 8," and seldom missed a state Legion convention. This is where my story really begins.

Eddie began to be known for his colorful costumes and his goat during the Legion conventions. One tale was noted with a picture and story in a local newspaper in 1938 about his run-in with the Ware police on his trek to the convention in Worcester, Massachusetts. He was in Ware about noon with his goat and was "attired in his customary rig of a varied assortment of colors and huge straw hat with his cane." He was stopped by the police "because of the lack of noticeable reason for his hike through town" and was asked for his permit for advertising. He showed his delegate's card for the convention and was allowed to proceed towards Worcester.

Eddie Parent, the popcorn man.

In 1941 Eddie decided to give a well-earned rest to his goat, Billy, who had accompanied him to conventions for twelve years, and hit upon the idea of using a turkey to take to conventions. He went to the Holland Turkey Farm on Old Enfield Road and picked out a turkey he named Pete. He thought Pete offered the best possibilities for a good act. Eddie, who was representing the Hampshire County Voiture, District 484 of the "40 and 8," also decided to change the outmoded fashions he had worn in previous years and would be attired in Russian pajamas. No explanation as to why the change, but once again he made headlines.

Eddie died in June of 1942. While there are other stories that could be told of Eddie Parent—his membership in the local Democratic committee, his campaign to elect Michael Curley as governor, and his promotion of all kinds of sports—I will close with comments written by Lewis Blackmer in his obituary in the *Sentinel*:

> *Belchertown lost a bit of its distinctiveness on Monday with the passing of Edward B. Parent. His popcorn wagon at the south end of the Common had gotten to be a sort of landmark, replacing in sentiment somewhat the old well by which it stood. And he sold not only popcorn, but poetry—bits of verse written out of real experience with life, by Mrs. Charles W. Clark, with whose family he lived for 37 years. Then, of course, he was the colorful member of the American Legion, attending regularly the big conventions, where for some years, he crashed the headlines and the comics with his trained billy goat, which was the counterpart of Mary's Little Lamb.*

> *Doris Dickinson*

BELCHERTOWN COMMUNITY HALL

Tag sales, the Belchertown Fair and recent holiday bazaars have brought people to the Common during the past several months. While making the tour of the bazaars, I visited the building that was the St. Francis Church. I had visited the building earlier in the summer during the St. Francis tag sale. As I entered it again, I was struck by the bareness of the interior, bereft of its religious artifacts since the church's move to its new location. I spoke with several people about my concern on what would eventually happen to the building. Both had heard that movies had once been shown in the building. Movies had been shown in the building in the past, but that was only one phase of its existence. This historic building has a long and interesting history.

The building was erected in 1836 at the expense of five thousand dollars as the Brainerd Church. The Brainerd Church was organized in September 1834 as a reaction to a movement within the Congregational Church against the Masonic Lodge. Many of the men who formed the Brainerd Church refused to renounce their membership in the Lodge. Most of these men were the "pillars" of the Congregational Church at that time. Sixty-eight members withdrew their church membership to form the new organization. The Brainerd Church grew to about 180 members.

In early January 1841, there was a movement towards the rejoining of the churches and societies. Mark Doolittle, in his history of the Congregational Church said, "The causes which seven years before had led to a division of the church, seem to have melted away and a state of united feeling, favorable to the prosperity of the church by a union succeeded."

The next tenant of this building was the Baptist Church. They purchased the building from the Brainerd Church in 1842. Their old meetinghouse, erected in 1814 and located on Maple Street, needed considerable repairs. The Baptist Church, organized in 1796, existed for 117 years and has a long and interesting history, but that will have to be told another time. The church disbanded about 1913. The townspeople back then must have been wondering, as I have been, what would be the next transition for this old building.

An advertisement for movies at the Community Hall, later the St. Francis Church.

The Belchertown Board of Trade was active during this period and appointed a committee to look into securing the building for a community hall. The committee, working with other members and the *Sentinel*, secured pledges for about $1,400 and this amount was considered sufficient to make a start. An option on the Baptist Church property was secured in 1916, and plans for a permanent organization were made. The Belchertown Community League was incorporated and changes were started on the building to adapt it to the needs of an entertainment hall. Outside of the auditorium, the changes included the removal of the old belfry, the construction of a ticket office and adding a fire escape. The state police gave a permit allowing the auditorium to be used for entertainment, putting the capacity at 250 for the main part and 25 for the stage. A new heating system was needed. By 1917 enough shares in the corporation had been paid to allow the building to be wired for electricity, and a moving picture machine and a "reflectoscope" had been purchased. The records of this organization, as well as the records of the Baptist church, are preserved in the archives of the Stone House Museum.

For over six years, movies were shown and the hall was used for community events and entertainments. It was used a number of times during World War I, when government loans were being put over and the war spirit was being promoted. The hall came the nearest to meeting the desires of its promoters when the community club fitted up a meeting room in the basement and planned to render community service in the matter of restrooms, the dispensing of school lunches, etc. However, in November 1921, the burning of the high school building on Maple Street made it imperative to abandon this project, as the space was needed for temporary school purposes and three rooms were outfitted for the town's use.

With the nearing of the completion of Lawrence Memorial Hall and the new high school, the directors of the Community League began questioning whether the town could support as many public buildings as it would shortly have. With this in mind, and the faltering finances of the venture, they sold the property to the Roman Catholic Diocese for use as a church in November of 1922 for $12,000. The Catholic Mission was in urgent need of a church building and, as the *Sentinel* said, "not only by reason of their growing constituency locally, but in some measure by the coming of the State School. The new owners are setting to work at once to put the building in condition for use and will, no doubt, make it an attractive property." St. Francis Church was dedicated in June 1923 and was in service for eighty-two years until the new church building was erected on Jabish Street. The building and the rectory are still in use by the parish. What will the future bring for this building that has seen so much history pass through its doors?

Doris Dickinson

CHANGES IN TOWN

Anyone driving through Belchertown must wonder what is happening in town. Buildings are being demolished almost overnight and construction of new buildings is evident everywhere. What is not so evident is the loss of history, the history behind those homes and the families that lived in those homes. Seeing all these changes that are taking place all over Belchertown, I began to recall and to research some of people and places that have been lost forever.

The little house that was demolished on State Street across from Checkers to make way for Country Bank was owned by George Greene in the early 1930s. Hubert Greene, his son, remembers digging out the cellar under the house by hand with shovel, bucket and wheelbarrow. He also dug a well and put in a septic system. He planted some of the trees that are still standing. When the railroad bridge was rebuilt in 1949, the new road went right through the middle of their property. The barn was on one side and the house on the other. The family raised chickens as did many Belchertown families during the thirties. His mother and a friend started a restaurant to be called "Millies" across the street from the house. The week the restaurant was to open, Greene's mother died and one week later, her friend passed away as well. The restaurant, later owned by Richard Ramadon, became known as Daisy Mae's. Daisy Mae's, then owned by Chester Dowd, burned down in 1971. Jackson and Harrington built another restaurant and office building called the Red Pantry. That building now houses Kristina's Bakery and Restaurant. This is just a thumbnail sketch of the history that surrounded that little house.

There have been many changes on North Main Street. Where the new fire station is located, once stood the home of Dr. Estes Howe, a physician during the Revolutionary War. It is said that General Lafayette visited Dr. Howe at his home when he visited Belchertown in 1825. That house burned, along with five other buildings during what the newspaper termed a "great conflagration" in 1899. This fire, ironically, is what started the movement for the formation of a fire company and the push for a municipal water supply.

Loman Smith, an undertaker, then built a house on the site in the early 1900s. That house, which was purchased by the town as a site for the new fire station, was moved down on Federal Street in 1987.

The town's first fire station was moved across the street to its present site on North Main Street. Elijah Pepper had built a small house on this property about 1843. He was employed by the Filer Carriage Manufactory, which was just up the street and was on land owned by Mr. Filer. The house, a small dwelling, was what might have been called a workingman's cottage and was typical of others erected in town during the nineteenth century. Similar houses were built on Jackson Street for men working in the carriage industry. The Beers and Story Funeral Home bought the property and demolished the house.

During 1989 another old house was demolished for the building of Cold Spring Commons. This was the home of William and Marion Shaw. The house was built about 1835 by Josiah Cowles who was a carriage manufacturer. William Shaw was town clerk, treasurer and collector for many years. He wrote *The History of Belchertown in the Eighteenth Century*, which is one of the very few books ever published covering the history of the town. Marion Shaw taught in the Belchertown schools for thirty-three years and shared her husband's love of history. Every year her sixth-grade class studied Belchertown history and wrote papers about various aspects of the town's past. These papers were compiled in a booklet. Some of the booklets made by her students now reside in the archives of the Stone House Museum. She was a very popular teacher. It's too bad that more of this is not done in the schools today to give students a sense of the history of their town.

A house that was recently demolished to make way for the Jonquil Estates on North Main Street was the house I knew as the Fred Thayer home. Fred raised chickens and sold eggs. He was a Friday night visitor—with a dozen or so eggs—at our home on South Main Street for many years. He sometimes had a bit of news or a joke and always a smile. His house was built about 1860 by Alfred H. Hill. Hill was listed in the business directory on the 1860 map of Belchertown as the operator of a meat and provision store, though probably not on this site. The house was owned by the Charles Sanford family for over twenty years and by the Thayer family from 1944 to 1980.

Smitty's Rock and Wood Motel.

The landscape of North Main Street changed dramatically with the moving of what was known for many years as the Chadbourne home and the building of McDonald's. This house faced demolition but was saved by a group of investors. It was moved down North Main Street and onto land purchased on Daniel Shays Highway to become business and office space. The house was built circa 1785 by Nathan Parsons Jr. He was a merchant and built this imposing large two-story colonial home. It was later the home of Amos Mason who purchased acreage abutting on the south in 1799. Lloyd Avenue and Chadbourne Road were laid out on this land in the 1950s and new homes were built. Changes have even occurred for some of these homes and two are now business establishments.

A house that is slowly being demolished on Federal Street to make way for condominiums was built about 1853 by Amos F. Clark, great-great-grandfather of Shirley Bock. Mr. Clark was a carpenter, wagon maker and blacksmith. His blacksmith shop stood on the side front yard. This house was later the home of the Edward Parson family who had moved here from Enfield, Massachusetts, when their home was demolished for the building of Quabbin Reservoir. The barn and outbuildings were used for their egg business.

The house and barn on the corner of North Main Street and Route 9 seems to be facing the same fate as others. A hearing was scheduled by the Planning Board last week to review a site plan for the erection of another bank. This old house was built about 1820. The first owner of the dwelling was Simeon Pepper, one of the men active in Belchertown's famous carriage industry. He also at one time served the town as selectman. The house has been altered over the years and was most recently a rental property. It sits, windows boarded, awaiting its fate.

We also keep watch of the little purple building at the intersection that is boarded up and slated, I'm sure, for demolition soon. It will be the site of the North Brookfield Savings Bank. This building has had a varied past. It was erected by Henry R. Berger in 1946. He served lunches and ice cream and also sold fresh fruits and vegetables. He used two little buildings that were already on the site for building materials. Ruthella (Conkey) Tucker said that the house just past the intersection going towards Ware was moved from that site to its present location with the construction of Daniel Shays Highway. Perhaps the two buildings had belonged to that house. In 1948 Mr. and Mrs. Alexis Therault took over and operated the business as the Four Corners Grill for many years. Many townspeople remember Al and Edie. It was a gathering place. Its last transformation was as a garden shop.

Nearby, where a long line of cars stop each morning for their donuts and coffee, once stood a home built by Captain Charles Dunbar. He built the house about 1810 as a two-full-story, Federal-style dwelling. The main portion was one room deep with a single story ell. The property remained in the Dunbar family for nearly a century. It was originally a one-hundred acre homestead extending beyond Jabish Brook. The construction of Daniel Shays Highway divided the property and, at that time, an underground cattle crossing was built so the cows could come and go to the pastures. Remnants of this crossing still exist. The property was purchased in 1935 from H.W. Conkey by Paul Squires who built a Shell gas station and general store at the intersection. Later, in 1939 he built the first tourist cabins in those pastures along Daniel Shays Highway. The gas station went through several ownerships and renovations over the years and finally evolved into the present convenience store.

The last use of the old Dunbar house was the Village Package and General Store and the Quabbin Bait Shop. The house was demolished in 1989 to make way for Belchertown Crossing. Ironically the Bank of New England was interested at the time in locating a bank on the site of the old Dunbar house, but this never came to pass. I wonder if they rue that decision. I think there may have been only two banks in town at that time.

The six tourist cabins that Paul Squires built in 1939 existed until a few short years ago. They were operated by Henry Berger for a while, and in 1952 they were purchased by Mr. and Mrs. Edward Schmidt. An Around Our Town column in the *Sentinel* in 1964 had this to say: "They added new units in the back, connected the original cabins and built the center portion that contains the office and eight units. A total of 18 units now comprise the Smitty's Motel." The motel was faced with native stone and still stands, but is now filled with local business establishments. The little wooden cabins in back were burned by the fire department several years ago.

This "nearby history" has been gathered from various sources; from newspaper articles, research done by others, discussions with people who have memories of some of these changes, photographs and even an old postcard. I would be remiss, if I didn't give credit for the information about these early homes to a group of people who back in the late 1970s and early '80s took it upon themselves to start documenting the history of the buildings in Belchertown. The Belchertown Historical Commission—then composed of Gerald G. Tremaine, chairman; Shirley Bock; Suzanne Bay; Robert J. Hansbury; Mark A. Nickerson; and assisted by Helen Lister, curator of the Stone House Museum; several federal employees hired under the Comprehensive Employment and Training Act (CETA); and others—started the deed and historical research. This research ultimately led to the listing of the center of town on the National Historic Register in 1982. They also published a very valuable resource book in 1982 entitled *Along the County Road: Belchertown Discovered*, which covers many of the properties that have been mentioned in this article. I can't help but wonder how a future writer, say a hundred years from now, will gather her information about the changes that will have taken place in Belchertown.

Doris Dickinson

More Changes

Another bit of history is gone. In a day, the house at the corner of Route 9 and 202 was demolished. This is the fourth structure to be demolished near this busy intersection over the past several years. The house was built in the early 1820s by Simeon Pepper. He was a selectman from 1836 to 1838. Later on, it was known as the Dunbar place.

One more change needs mentioning. Sitting on a little knoll just past the old stone mile marker on Route 9 and George Hannum Road was a house that was built sometime before 1795. Ebenezer Warner was its first owner. Records show that Ebenezer and his son, Elisha, were inn holders in Belchertown in 1783 and 1787, but it is not known whether that building was their inn. It is certain, however, that Ebenezer sold this house in 1794 to the Robert Dunbar family and that Captain Azel Dunbar kept a tavern there until 1815. Down through the years, the tavern was owned and operated by a number of people. Later owners farmed the extensive acreage. It was owned by the Quabbin Development Company as a rental property in 1988 when it was destroyed late at night by a disastrous fire. It had stood almost two hundred years on that site. The house was not rebuilt, and the land lay fallow until the Stop and Shop was built last year.

Federal Street, back in the early 1800s, was the site of the first carriage shops in Belchertown. Simeon Pepper formed the Belchertown Carriage Manufactory with Mason Abbey and Harrison Holland on Federal Street. Along the road were several taverns and inns, blacksmith shops, small stores and a ropewalk. The first post office was in Elisha Warner's tavern. He was the first Belchertown postmaster appointed in 1797 during the presidency of George Washington.

There was a town meeting called in 1789 to see where a new church was to be built. In the early days, the meetinghouse was the focus of all community interests; here, all religious services, town meetings and political gatherings were held within the same walls. A site on Federal Street, near Ebenezer Warner's, was proposed along with a site in the center of town "near the schoolhouse." The center site won out. After several carriage manufactories burned down and were not rebuilt, the carriage industry moved to the center of town and Federal Street lost out as a business center.

There is an old saying: what goes around comes around. Almost two hundred years later, this area is once again a busy site. Instead of wagons and buggies, we now see cars, trucks and buses. Instead of taverns, blacksmith shops and carriage manufactories, we have Stop and Shop, McDonald's, Subway, Dunkin Donuts and, so far, three banks.

Doris Dickinson

Winter

Skating on the Common

Skating on the Common has been a favorite pastime over the years. The Belchertown Fire Department has usually been at the forefront of whatever group wanted to spearhead the flooding of the Common. Since the flooding on the north end of the Common for the Year 2000 celebration, the maintenance of the rink has been continued. Driving by the Common, you can see children and families once again enjoying this winter pastime.

Skating on the Common.

Back in 1963, the late Dr. Kenneth Collard was interested in seeing that a safe skating rink be provided for the children. Just before Christmas, he announced that the skating rink on the north end of the Common should be in use for a week or ten days. He said this was made possible by the combined efforts of many people, including Lawrence Bowser, Loren Shumway, William Lincourt, John Plowucha, Richard McGinnis and Edward Fuller. The Belchertown Firemen's Auxiliary had been largely responsible for the flooding of the rink. They worked under the direction of some of the regular firemen: Donald Bock, Raymond Menard, Albert Dewhurst, Harry Brougham, Elwyn Bock and Edward Gates. Lights were installed by Edward Czech and the night lighting was provided by the police department. The rink was kept plowed by Leon Capen and Edward Gates, and several benches were loaned by Mr. and Mrs. Saul Nulman. It was a community effort.

In earlier years, the rink was usually at the south end of the Common, but in the late 1950s the town voted to place a parking lot at the south end and that moved the rink to the north end of the Common.

Doris Dickinson

Blake Jackson's Memories

We each have stories to tell. I was recently transcribing some handwritten pages from the archives of the Stone House Museum that gave some insight into what life was like growing up in Belchertown. They were written by Blake Jackson. Sadly, the story was never finished, but the few pages that he wrote on yellow ruled paper give a wonderful glimpse of the years; he wrote on the opening page: "This little narrative is an account of my boyhood days in Belchertown during the period 1903 to 1917. A wonderful period of time in New England. It is written to give an idea of how small town America lived at the time. It must be remembered that we had no hard surfaced roads, no electricity..."

He tells of his home on Walnut Street (now Jackson Street); the chores that he, his brothers and his sisters were assigned; the bakery his father owned; and his first ride in a car, an Oldsmobile that had a curved dash and a tiller, not a steering wheel. Although he never finished the story, he had made an outline of what he wanted to include. That outline covers four pages on the computer. It is a wonderful compendium of people, events and places during those early days at the turn of the century. Maybe at some future date, we can print those few handwritten pages in the *Sentinel*, but for now I will share what he wrote about delivering papers.

A newsboy hawks the *Saturday Evening Post* outside of Jackson's store.

I had a paper route covering about 3½ miles. I would meet the 6:20 milk train at the station, ride down Depot Hill [Maple Street] in my cart on the sidewalk. The cart had roller bearings in the wheels and a brake on one rear wheel. No rubber tires and I apparently made a noise going down the hill—did go pretty fast—as Charles Clark, the barber, said he knew it was time to get up when he heard me go down the hill. I would leave the papers at my father's store, fill my bag, get on my bicycle and deliver to houses on South Main St., down as far as Capt. Anderson's, later George Scott's house and then Clarence Morey's. Then deliver on Jabish St., Park Street and Main Street and finish up on Walnut St., have my breakfast and go to school by 9 a.m. In the winter I would use my sled, slide down Depot Hill in the road as the snow would be packed nicely by the horse drawn sleds and then walk the rest of my route—some mornings about zero and deep snow—one woman used to ask me to come in by the stove for a minute to get warm. Later a town ordinance was passed that forbid riding a bicycle on the town sidewalks. This would have made it very difficult for me on my paper route and I saw Dr. Francis Austin, chairman of the selectmen, and told him my problem and he gave me a permit to ride on the sidewalks when delivering my papers but warned me not to ride at any other time.

Blake Jackson was born in Belchertown in 1901, the son of John W. and Sarah

Porter Jackson. His father had opened Jackson's Store on Main Street in the old Farmer's Bank building in 1893. They also had a bakery on Walnut Street. When his father died in 1931, Blake took over the store. He owned the business for twenty-seven years and then sold it in 1958 to become a stockbroker. He died in 1985. There are so many stories that could be told about John W. Jackson, Blake and Jackson's Store. Both were photographers, leaving behind a legacy of photos that chronicle the changes in Belchertown over the years.

Doris Dickinson

CLARK AND JACKSON COLLECTIONS

The Belchertown Historical Association recently received two important additions to the photograph collection in the archives. The Clark Collection is a gift from Charles Clark Jr. and the Jackson Collection is a gift from Mrs. George Jackson. The old cliché that a picture is worth a thousand words may be a little farfetched, but pictures do add a dimension to history that cannot be denied.

The late Charles Clark Jr. was a grandson of Samuel and Mabel (Freeman) Stevenson and lived for most of his life at the family home just off Maple Street. He was the son of Charles Clark, a barber in town for many years, and Margaret Stevenson. His collection of family and town photographs represents a period of Belchertown history that spans from the late 1800s to the 1940s. His grandfather, Samuel Stevenson, arrived in Belchertown at about fifteen years of age, shortly after the Civil War ended. He died in 1927 and his obituary gave a short synopsis of his life:

> *Sam Stevenson, 78, was born in slavery, although he had no recollection of actual servitude. He became an orderly for Adj. Harry Walker of the First Connecticut regiment when it was stationed in Baltimore. He followed the regiment throughout the war. At its close he brought Adj. Walker's horses to this town and had made his home here since…Mr. Stevenson was for over 40 years in the family of the late Dr. George Thomson. He married Miss Mabel Freeman of this town.*

The Jackson Collection also spans a period of Belchertown history. George Jackson and John Jackson were brothers. John Jackson arrived in Belchertown around 1891. He was a butter maker and started creameries in Connecticut and Massachusetts including Belchertown. He also owned Jackson's Store, a fixture on

Main Street for many years. He was a photographer and his glass-plate negatives are in the collection at the Stone House. He was also president of the Belchertown Historical Association from 1925 until his death in 1931. His son, Blake Jackson, who took over the store upon the death of his father, was also a well-known photographer and a member of the Belchertown Color Camera Club. The Stone House archive is the repository of some of his work, especially the photos documenting changes on Main Street. Blake Jackson was a trustee of the historical association.

George Jackson's death in 1931 followed closely on that of his brother, John Jackson. He had learned the butter-making trade from his brother. He came to Belchertown in 1893 to work in the store, becoming manager of the Belchertown Creamery in 1900. He worked there until it closed in 1917. Upon the completion of Lawrence Memorial Hall in 1923, he became the caretaker of the Belchertown schools, a position he held until his death. His son, Bob Jackson, who wrote the "Steeple" column for many years for the *Belchertown Sentinel*, wrote a number of articles about his father, the Belchertown Creamery and the local schools. Bob Jackson was also a trustee of the Belchertown Historical Association.

These collections are currently being catalogued and researched. Many

Charlie Clark as a toddler.

photographs have names, but many do not. Unlocking the history of old photographs entails researching family history, locations, time frames, clothing and hairstyles and understanding the types of photographs. I love old photographs and old documents. It makes the people that I have only read about come alive. Our archival holdings in the Stone House have continued to grow thanks to generous individuals willing to donate collections. Without our repository and others like them, our past would be lost. We share a common purpose—to preserve and protect our history and to provide materials for current users and future researchers.

Doris Dickinson

Ruby Knight's Autograph Book

B its of history show up in many places. Several weeks ago, a friend called up to say that his mother had found something on eBay that had a Belchertown connection. It was an autograph book that had been owned by Ruby F. Knight with autographs from Belchertown people from the late 1890s to 1905. She was asked to bid on the article and it has arrived at the Stone House Museum. Another bit of Belchertown history was back home to be added to the archives at the museum.

Ruby Knight was born in Belchertown in 1874 and attended Belchertown schools. The autograph book probably was used during her high school days. It has the names of her high school friends.

Ruby started teaching school in Belchertown in 1891, probably right after graduation. She taught for one session of ten weeks at Chestnut Hill district school at $5.00 a week. By 1900, she was again teaching at Chestnut Hill, but her salary had increased to $6.50 and she taught for thirty weeks and was paid $195. Through the years, she taught in six district schools and was principal of Center Grade School for ten years until her retirement in 1936. She was principal during part of the time that her cousin, Herman Knight, was superintendent of schools. When she retired, Edith Towne, her high school classmate, also retired as eighth grade teacher at the high school. Edith had started teaching the same year. Together they had taught almost a century in Belchertown schools. Ruby Knight died at the age of eighty-eight in 1962.

Miss Knight was the daughter of Charles Sumner and Flavilla Bennett Knight. They lived in the Turkey Hill section of Belchertown. The parents named all of their children for precious stones. In addition to Ruby, there was her sister, Garnet, and her three brothers, Jewel Bennett Knight, Charles Pearl Knight and Jasper M. Knight.

Ruby's autograph book now joins other autograph books that have been given to the Stone House over the years. These books are filled with names, verses and sometimes drawings. I wonder if students today have their friends and teachers write in autograph books. I still have one that goes back sixty-four years to when I was graduating from eighth grade at Roosevelt Jr. High School in Oklahoma City. It brings back memories.

Doris Dickinson

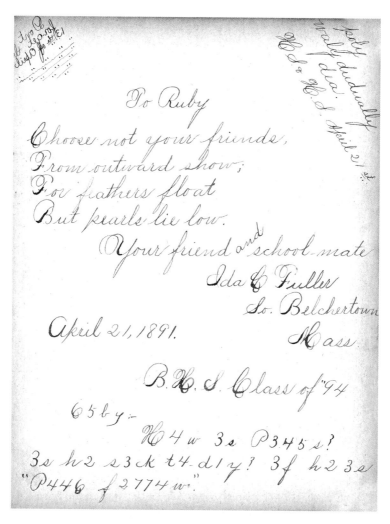

A page from Ruby Knight's autograph book.

My Flexible Flyer

Just after the big December snowstorm, I saw kids and some parents sliding in the sloped field at the corner of George Hannum and Hamilton Streets. They were using all kinds of snow vehicles. Some were a kind of uncontrollable plastic bowls. Even cardboard was used as a makeshift sled. To me this wasn't the most thrilling use of snow, even though they seemed to be having a good time.

Now, allow me to go back to the 1920s and '30s, when we used to slide down Jackson Street from the top, where it meets Main Street, sometimes all the way to the railroad crossing. The only trouble with that long slide was the fact that we had to walk back with our sleds. We always had a place to get warm and have some hot cocoa, either at my grandmother's house or across the street at the Spencers'. In those days, streets were plowed just enough for a car to get through with chains on the rear wheels. Sanding and salting were done sparingly, if at all. There was very little traffic and it moved slowly. The packed down snow made a perfect surface for sleds. On special occasions some of the older kids brought a double rip. These rips were usually homemade and consisted of two heavy-duty sleds connected by a plank eight feet or more in length. The rear sled was fixed and the front was steerable (more or less). Quite often, we wound up in the ditch or over the snowbank. They were fast and a little dangerous, but with the right conditions and a good driver, we got a thrilling ride. Today the rip would not pass the child safety standards. I am still amazed how we got out of our childhoods alive. I would venture to guess that the rip was a precursor of the four-man bobsled of Olympic fame.

I was fortunate to have a Flexible Flyer, which was at that time the Cadillac of sleds. It was fifty-one inches in length, steerable and streamlined. The ends of the runners curved back gracefully into the fame, giving it an appearance of speed when it was just sitting there. It could easily accommodate two riders, either sitting or stacked. I liked stacked—that is, a girl on top keeping my back warm. But I digress; I'm talking about a great sled, here.

Wondering if they had become an antique, like a Model T Ford, I went to the Internet and discovered they are still available. They were made in China (surprise, surprise) for the remnants of the original manufacturer, but production stopped in 1999. The last ones made there were exactly the same as mine. It appears that they are still available, as one website listed them for seventy dollars. I also discovered the sleds were invented by one Samuel Allen in the 1880s and a patent was granted in August 1889. The first sleds he tried to market were called "Fairy Coasters" and were not a success. Then in the early 1900s, the sleds became a hit and could not be manufactured fast enough.

When we sold our old South Main Street home and moved to Pine Valley, we had to get rid of a lot of our stuff, so the sled had to go. We gave the Flyer to Brandon and Andrew Leighton, a couple of boys we regard as adopted grandchildren. We kept an old small sled that my wife, Doris, uses as part of a Christmas decoration for our front yard. When we were talking about sleds, Doris casually said that this one was a Flexible Flyer. I didn't buy it, but off to the shed she went and returned to inform me that she was right. (She usually is.)

I mentioned to my friend and former Sunday school teacher that I was writing about sliding on Jackson Street. I will call her J.S., here. She remembered sliding on Jackson Street with her boyfriend, whom I will call A.S. She revealed that occasionally they would veer off. She gave me no details of this "veering," but being a Sunday school teacher, I am sure there was no hanky-panky involved.

My Flexible Flyer lives on, but sliding on Jackson Street is but a sweet memory.

Harvey Dickinson

AD MOORE

I continue to be amazed, but gratified, that pieces of Belchertown history keep arriving at the Stone House Museum. It usually starts with a telephone call from someone asking if we would be interested in materials from a Belchertown family. This has happened twice recently. What makes it even more interesting is that both families lived, at one time, on Jackson Street. This piece is about the Addison Moore family.

The first call was from Gordon Douty in Monson, Massachusetts. He had some photographs from the Moore family, who once lived in the Turkey Hill section of town. In 1920 George H.B. Green, a longtime resident of Turkey Hill wrote a series of articles for the *Sentinel* about the early residents of that section of town. He wrote:

> *The place came into the possession of Addison D. Moore, Sr. who built up an extensive trade in moss goods, window decorations and other artistic novelties. For several years under the name of A. D. Moore and Co. a thriving business was conducted here. They erected a good sized workshop and employed several hands, both in the shop and in collecting moss, etc., for miles around. The family was peculiarly adapted to this work. A daughter, with much artistic ability and skill, would design and paint pictures of the proposed decorations, the father with great patience and close attention to detail, would build the models and necessary patterns, while the mother, with her book of designs, her pleasing address and wonderfully persuasive tongue would take the road as saleswoman. She did what I believe no one else could do. Her field was large and her list of customers included such houses as Siegel, Cooper and Co. of New York, Marshal Field and Co. of Chicago, Jordan Marsh and Co. of*

Boston, and the leading firms of Philadelphia, Baltimore and other cities. To them and others she sold window decorations, the prices of some which reached above the $ 1,000 figure. One Chicago firm even sent her a check for $300 to pay her expenses to that city and return that she might inspect their windows and design something especially for them. The receipts from the business were good; the expenses, too, were heavy and the profits were not commensurate with the labor and worry involved.

This article from the *Sentinel*, a small newspaper article, some photographs and some of the creations and decorations are all that remain of this very interesting early business.

Perhaps some people will still remember the son, a local entrepreneur, Addison Moore Jr., better known as Ad. He lived on Jackson Street with his wife, Frances Fletcher. In 1911 he started an ice cream plant in Turkey Hill, later moving it to Palmer, where it became known as the Forest Lake Dairies. In 1919 he was in the ice business, cutting ice on Greenwich Lake in the Swift River Valley (now Quabbin Reservoir). But, perhaps he will best be remembered for designing and building what was Belchertown's—and maybe the area's—first recreational vehicles. He built the first about 1920 and drove it to Florida in 1922. It was the prototype of several things he was to build. He named it Blue Heaven. His trips were made, usually with a traveling companion, during the days when there were few camping areas along the way south. He wrote letters to the *Sentinel* about their adventures. These were colorful accounts of the people he met, the weather, the countryside and the interest in his vehicle and its conveniences. It even had a back porch!

In the 1920s, Ad Moore built this recreational vehicle, called Blue Heaven, for his trips to Florida.

The pictures of the Moore family members, their homes and the Blue Heaven given to us by Mr. Douty, add another piece of history to the archives of the Stone House Museum. We are grateful that people think of the Belchertown Historical Association as a repository for preserving Belchertown history for future generations.

Doris Dickinson

ED AND ELEANOR SCHMIDT

Previously, I wrote about the Moore family who lived on Jackson Street. This story is about the Schmidt family who also, for a time, lived on Jackson Street. A telephone call came from Kenneth Griswold of Hatfield, who had some materials from the Eleanor Schmidt estate. He wanted to know if we at the Belchertown Historical Association would be interested. He arrived with two boxes and a basket filled with mostly photographs, audiotapes and thirty-five-millimeter slides. Generally, when materials arrive at the Stone House Museum, we try to learn more about the history of each family and its connection to Belchertown. So, the research begins and the story unfolds. But it is never just one story; each story reveals many other stories about lives that are intertwined.

This story starts in the 1930s at Belchertown High School. Edward Schmidt Jr. of Belchertown and Eleanor Griswold of Prescott were classmates. This was during the days that high school students from the valley towns, now covered by the Quabbin Reservoir, were bused to Belchertown. Edward and Eleanor graduated in 1931 and were married in Amherst on September 16, 1939.

The Schmidt family first came to Belchertown when Edward Schmidt Sr. arrived here in the early 1900s. He resided on Jackson Street and was employed for a time in the bakery of John W. Jackson on Jackson Street. Later, he made his home on North Washington Street, where he operated a poultry farm. They had two sons, Edward Jr. and Albert. One of the articles given to the museum was an album of photographs of the damage done in Belchertown during the hurricane of 1938. Included in some of the ninety photographs, are some photos of the damage to the Schmidt Poultry Farm. After his retirement, Ed Schmidt Sr. and his wife, Grace, moved to Redondo Beach, California. On the death of Mr. Schmidt, Bob Jackson wrote,

> *The elder Schmidts were very active citizens of this town for many years. 'Smitty' was a big, jovial man, and a friend of all. He was baker for my Uncle John for a number of years, and like my uncle, was Master of the Vernon Lodge of Masons. Later, he became an energetic and very successful chicken farmer. These*

folks have always seemed a part of Belchertown, even though they had left us for far-away California.

Eleanor's family members were longtime residents of the town of Prescott. They were one of the many families that had to leave their home with the building of Quabbin Reservoir. The preserving of the history of the Quabbin Valley became one of the passions of her life.

When I came to Belchertown in 1945, Eleanor had a photography studio at her home on Jackson Street. She was a great photographer and was known for her photos that were used on Christmas cards. We have photographs she took of our family when our two oldest daughters were small. I am sure that other families in Belchertown must have similar pictures. Some of the photographs we received for the Stone House archives were of that era, including some of the Schmidts' Christmas cards of their son.

While doing my research, I became aware of how many homes Ed and Eleanor shared and built in Belchertown. Besides their home on Jackson Street, they lived, at different times, in three homes on Ware Road. One was a unique home they built that is now the Quabbin Animal Hospital. They bought the home of Lewis Blackmer, off Cottage Street, but probably never lived there. The many residents who patronize the business establishments located at the Village Square on Route 202 might be surprised to learn that the building started out as Smitty's Rock and Wood Motel. Built by the Schmidts, it was the first modern motel in Belchertown.

Eleanor Schmidt and friend.

It reflected Ed's love of rock in the façade, with the stonework done by Paul Rufo of Belchertown. They bought the property in 1952 where Paul Squires had built some "tourist cabins." They began the expansion and remodeling that resulted in the motel, and Eleanor managed the business until it was sold in 1966 to Kamin's, Inc.

Eleanor then turned to local politics. She decided to seek the office of selectman in 1969. She was concerned about the rising property taxes that were "forcing some residents to sell their property." Edward Gates and Francis P. Loftus also sought the three-year seat on the board. With 736 votes cast in the election, she received 464 votes, almost double the votes cast for her opponents. She served until 1972. Eleanor became the second woman to be elected to the board in the history of the town. Marjorie Tilton, elected in 1945, was the first.

Their son, Louis, better known as "Cy," was born in 1940. Like his parents, he graduated from Belchertown High School and also graduated in 1963 from the University of Massachusetts with a degree in food service. He worked at the Cain's pickle factory in South Deerfield and, in the last four years of his life, at the All Star Dairy in South Hadley. He married Elizabeth Theriault of Belchertown.

Cy's story is one that could stand alone. He was born with cystic fibrosis, which was confirmed when he was fourteen years old. He became part of a research study group of this baffling disease. Cy died on February 5, 1969, but he had lived to be one of the oldest cystic fibrosis patients in the world.

At his death, Eleanor wrote a thank you letter to the people of Belchertown for their support over the years. She wrote, in part,

> *Life for Cy meant living each day one at a time. Each day he took an enormous amount of medication…He went to work each day and did a man's work no matter what the weather—just happy to be alive. Cy was an avid reader, he challenged everything, yet he had a great deal of compassion and understanding. He loved chemistry and all things mechanical…We will continue his fight for him because you cared enough to share.*

Eleanor, born in the former Quabbin Valley town of Prescott, lived in Belchertown for over sixty years. She was a founding member and former president of the Prescott Historical Society, which later merged with Swift River Valley Historical Society. She was its representative on the citizens' advisory committee for Quabbin, regarding policies for the Metropolitan District Commission at the Quabbin Reservoir.

She was instrumental in raising the funds and arranging the move of the North Prescott Methodist Episcopal Church from Orange to New Salem to the grounds of the Swift River Valley Historical Society. To many, she was the spokesperson for the Quabbin Valley that was. She had been interviewed and videotaped many times. She also taped interviews with many of the former residents.

Edward Schmidt died in March of 1985, and Eleanor Griswold Schmidt, age eighty, died at her home on Ware Road in January 1994. They are buried with their son at Quabbin Park Cemetery. Eleanor left her estate to the Swift River Valley Historical Society. One of the interesting stipulations of her will was for the historical societies surrounding the Quabbin Reservoir. Each society would receive a yearly stipend if they made a banner representing their society and carried the banner each year in the Memorial Day Parade at the Quabbin Park Cemetery. Members of the Belchertown Historical Association proudly carry their banner each year and march in the parade. I think she was making sure that the former residents of the Quabbin Valley would be remembered in the future.

As I wrote in the beginning, a story has many stories that are woven around people, places and times. I have written only a few of the many that could be told. The legacy that has been given to the archives of the Stone House Museum will help to tell that story for many years to come.

Doris Dickinson

ALL-BELCHERTOWN CHRISTMAS PARTY

'Tis the season! For the past several weeks, the *Sentinel* has been full of notices for holiday parties and concerts. Main Street is once again decked with the lights we bought for the millennium celebration, the tree is lighted on the Common and homes are festooned with all kinds of decorations.

I want to tell you about another holiday season and another time—a time that was not so festive or joyful. The year was 1934—the middle of the Great Depression. The Depression started on October 29, 1929, with the crash of the stock market on what became known as Black Tuesday. It lasted all during the 1930s and only ended when the United States started gearing up for World War II in 1939. By 1932, 13 to 17 million workers were unemployed and Franklin D. Roosevelt had been elected president. He started many of his New Deal programs along with work and relief programs targeted toward the unemployed.

Articles in the *Sentinels* of the 1930s give evidence that the town was in the grip of the Depression and was receiving federal funds from the Civil Works Administration and the Works Progress Administration. One article tells of hiring local men to work on the roads at fifty cents an hour for a six-hour day and a five-day week. Belchertown during that era is a story in itself.

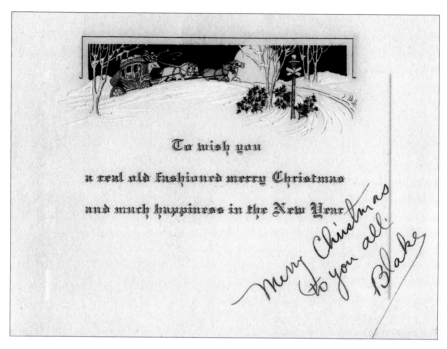

A Christmas card from Blake Jackson.

But this story is about a Christmas party—a party hailed as an All Belchertown Christmas and Distribution Party that was to be held in Lawrence Memorial Hall on December 21, 1934. It was free and open to everyone. A committee was appointed and plans were well underway in late November. Coin boxes were left in Hopkins' Store (located where Swift River Crafts is now) and the First National Store (where they now sell pizzas). Contributions came from local organizations such as Union Grange, Firemen, Eastern Star, Ladies Social Union, Boy Scouts, Junior League and the Teachers' Association. Most of these contributions were five dollars and under. Churches and individuals made contributions. The final collection was $112.86. That amount not only covered the expenses of the party, but thirty-five families in town were also remembered on Christmas day. The committee in charge of purchasing said, "considerable produce, canned goods, clothing, etc. contributed by townspeople helped out the purchasing committee quite materially. Local merchants made liberal gifts and concessions."

Come the night of the party, Memorial Hall was "jammed to the doors, with people standing in the vestibule and along the sides of the hall." Reverend Arthur Hope, pastor of the Congregational church, was program chairman. Schoolchildren from grades one through eight presented a program of carols, accompanied by Marion Shaw. The Methodist Church presented a play, *Beggars Charity*, and Lewis

Blackmer, editor of the *Sentinel*, gave a soliloquy. Santa then arrived and distributed boxes of candy. An orchestra had been hired for the evening, so the floor was cleared for dancing, many of the "old-time dances being sandwiched in" with Charles Austin as caller.

Aside from the orchestra (which came at a reduced price) and the candy, all services were contributed, even the services of the janitor. The school bus drivers "rendered a most valuable service in transporting school children."

During that time of little resources, everyone seemed to have contributed what they could and for the sum of $112.86 a community joined together in the spirit of giving for an All Belchertown Christmas Party.

Happy Holidays!

Doris Dickinson

FRIENDS CLOSER BY

B ack in the 1970s, Henry Renouf, former town moderator and owner of Robin Farm over on Swift River, wrote a column called Our Town for the *Sentinel*. Henry was a keen observer of the human condition and had a sharp and biting wit. He wrote a column back on December 22, 1977, which still resonates with me. I would like to share that column with you. He wrote:

> *I don't know whether to blame the terrific increase in the postal rates or the greater mobility of our liberated lifestyles for the difference, but it seems to me that we don't exchange as many Christmas greetings as we once did when the first class mail rate was 3 cents and when there were more homes and fewer houses. There was a time when address books lasted for years with but minor corrections while nowadays even a year-old address is likely to be obsolete.*
>
> *This was just a casual thought until, rummaging through a desk drawer the other day, I came upon a twenty-year-old list of names; people to whom I had sent Christmas cards in 1957. They were all old friends and as I read their names I felt guilty at having lost touch with them so completely. Not until several moments did it dawn on me that the fault was not mine. Their images were reflected so clearly in my mind's eye, their personalities so genuine and convincing, how could I believe that they are no longer with us?*
>
> *I saw "Doc" Austin proudly riding his spirited mount as marshal of our annual fair; Lewis Blackmer pounding his gavel at town meeting, trying to keep Elliott Cordner quiet; Carl Corliss delivering a registered letter all the way to*

Robin Farm; Earle Howland arguing that pound for pound, Jerseys are better than Holsteins; Romeo Joyal carefully sheltering an early shipment of baby chicks near the stove in the depot; Harold Ketchen wielding a butchers cleaver in one of his numerous businesses; Mike Mathras worrying over his chances at becoming the next selectman and, finally, smiling Harold Peck, with Belle looking over his shoulder, exchanging my first box of farm eggs for groceries.

These people are still alive and an essential part of me. Whether they all liked me or not is of no consequence. Life is not all roses and its most significant events cannot all be favorable. Our mixed up personalities are brewed from good and bad and what we treasure most is rarely best. And so I greet these old friends again in 1977 and wish them all a very Merry Christmas. Though their zip codes are unknown to me, I can always find them closer-by, as you, who knew them also can. They are and will remain a part of our reality as long as we live and for this alone we owe them thanks. And thanks we owe as well to those who still breathe our common air, both those we love and those with whom we share the problems of our day. A very Merry Christmas to you all from the bottom of our hearts.

I salute all those mentioned in this column. I knew them well; some better than others. I had lists like Henry, some with check marks, address changes, lines drawn

Henry Renouf and friend.

through names, but now I have them on my computer. With a quick stroke on the delete key, names disappear and addresses change, but like Henry, I still see them in my mind's eye. I can see Henry standing on the stage in Lawrence Memorial Hall (when it was large enough to hold everyone for a town meeting) gaveling down someone, saying, "Sit down, you are out of order." I can see his wife, Robin Renouf, who taught in the Belchertown schools. We shared Belchertown news gathering; she was writing for the morning *Springfield Union* and I for the afternoon *Springfield Daily News*. As Henry said in his closing, I can always find them closer by, as you, who knew them, always can.

Doris Dickinson

LUCK

He was called the "Iron Man" because he had played in over two thousand consecutive baseball games, a record that stood for fifty-six years. This day was to be the last time he would appear in uniform as a ball player and he was being honored at Yankee Stadium for having been the great player that he was. On that day, Lou Gehrig stood near home plate and when the tributes were over, he said these words: "Today, I consider myself the luckiest man on the face of the earth."

As the clangy echo of the old PA system punctuated his words, he and the sixty thousand fans at the stadium were aware that there was no hope for him to escape death from the ravages of amylateral sclerosis, the dreadful disease that was soon to bear his name. He was one of the great ball players of all time, cut down at the height of his career.

Most of us would call this turn of events bad luck, but Gehrig must have been referring to his life up to the time he was being honored and not his future. He was thinking of his luck of having attained the dream of many a young man of his day of wearing the uniform of the great New York Yankees. He had attained fame and fortune for in his career. He was paid as much as $39,000 a season, an astronomical amount of money in the Depression years of the thirties. Gehrig's outlook on his situation is to be admired and one that we all could adopt. Could any of us, knowing as Gehrig did of his pending death, call ourselves lucky?

We Americans have a lot of built-in good luck or a head start on good things, the very first being the fact that we live in America and in a community such as ours. We are in the enviable position of living in a relatively crime-free area. We have the advantage of a cultural atmosphere created by the area colleges. We have a high rate of employment and a stable economy. Most of us live in affluence compared to a large portion of the world. We can call this our common good luck.

A trade card for Curtis'
Blacksmith Shop.

In addition to the above, some of us have our personal luck such as a fine marriage and loving children and grandchildren, good health, a warm home and an adequate income.

It is said that you can make your good luck. Some people who seem to be plagued with bad luck have often created situations that bring on misfortune. In other words, they take chances that they don't have to take. Moderation in all we do lessens the chances of bad happenings.

We all are amused by the superstitions that concern luck—black cats, walking under ladders, broken mirrors and jinxes of all descriptions. There are rabbits' feet and talismans and hex signs. Most of us dismiss all these as silly, but when a cat crosses our path and it is black, somehow it makes a deeper impression on us than if it were a different color. We have all noticed sportsmen and women do curious antics as they start to compete. Many have their own little superstitions they believe bring them luck.

Some people do have just plain bad luck. All of us probably know at least one person who seems to have more than his share of tribulations. These persons are often fine and caring and have led prudent lives. Among these people you can find those whose bad luck has not affected their outlook and enthusiasm for life.

For those persons whose misfortunes are more than can be coped with, it is for us, the lucky ones, to share some of our good fortune. This can be done through governmental agencies, but they often fall short. Many people fall through the cracks; they must look to private groups such as the Salvation Army for help. Even then, there are still those who are hungry and homeless.

One of the basic tenets of the Christian church is to help those less fortunate than ourselves. I feel that is where we, as Christians, have failed miserably. It is hopeless to think that the government will ever be able to eradicate entirely hunger and homelessness. Some churches are doing a fine job on the problem, but I feel most are not addressing this issue.

So, as this New Year approaches, let us give thanks for our good luck and in the new year resolve to pay more heed to the needs of our less lucky fellow beings.

Harvey Dickinson

LARD

Is losing weight one of your New Years resolutions? If it is, you may have taken the new route of a low carbohydrate diet. This popular regimen calls for high protein food—meats, eggs and such—and most of the products of which other diets disapprove. Now, maybe lard will make a comeback.

A few years ago, before the big fire, I went to Besancon's Market and asked Ron, "Where do you hide the lard?" As well as I remember the conversation, it most likely went like this: "I didn't hide it. I don't stock it," he replied. "Whadda ya mean, you don't stock it? How can I make a pie without lard?" He came back with the "Nobody uses that stuff any more." Miffed, I went back home and made my pie with the stuff that rhymes with Frisco. Ron was probably right, for very few people use lard today, but some of us elders remember how good a pie crust tasted when it was made with lard, or doughnuts fried with it. I remember my Aunt Elsie's raised doughnuts—delicious!

I had a friend years ago who had relatives in Pennsylvania, and when he went to visit he would always bring me a large tin of potato chips that were fried in lard. Until a few years ago, chips were made in a storefront factory in Hyannis and distributed locally. My daughter, when visiting from Denver, always took back some of those "greasy chips," as she called them. The Hyannis company was later bought by a large food company, and they stopped making the chips with lard. I must admit that even now, they make a good chip. When the Wal-Mart Supercenter opened in Ware, they stocked a shelf with five-pound pails of lard. It was labeled "manteca"

(Spanish for lard), reflecting the merchandising of a different region. The pails soon disappeared when the management realized that Massachusetts is not big on five-pound pails of lard. Having traveled some in the Midwest and Southwest, I was aware that a lot of lard was used in their cooking. The Native Americans used it for their fried dough. Wal-Mart, along with the other supermarkets, still carries lard, but Checkers doesn't.

McDonald's, I have heard but can't prove, used a mix with lard for their french fries to improve the taste, until the nutrition terrorists found out and they were forced to stop the practice. Look up an old recipe for scratch soda biscuits and it will call for a mixture of lard and butter for shortening. It makes a big difference in the taste.

During the Great Depression in the 1930s, some of the poorer kids came to school with lard sandwiches. I can't say that was lip-smacking good, but I suppose it was better than nothing. At least the bread was home-baked. Salt pork was a staple at that time. Now, it seems to be used only to help flavor baked beans. It's hard to find all-fat salt pork—most comes prepackaged and has some lean meat in it. I'm talking about the way it was kept in a market in the old days, in a barrel of brine. When I can find some, I make myself a breakfast of eggs and fried salt pork. The pork is cut into one-eighth-inch strips and soaked in very hot water for a few seconds and then dredged in flour and fried. Most of the fat melts out as it browns. Now we are talking lip-smacking good!

They say it's bad for you. Lard clogs up your arteries. You know the saying—if something tastes bad, it's good for you. If it tastes good, it's bad for you—or now, maybe not.

Harvey Dickinson

GREEN PEPPERS

As I walk through Checkers or Randalls or Atkins market on a snowy day, I can't help but marvel at the fruit and vegetables available. They arrive from all over the world. Things are in season all year long. Just this past week, I bought a quart of strawberries and enjoyed strawberry shortcake, a delicacy that usually is reserved for late June and July. I also brought home some green peppers, bananas and salad fixins. We expect a well-stocked produce department and view this abundance with hardly a thought about the cost.

Looking back through some old "Steeple" columns, I came across one that Bob Jackson wrote in February 1959 about green peppers and their accessibility during the winter months. It seems that a hot lunch that snowy week in the Springfield school system had featured stuffed peppers. For thirty-five cents you received a large stuffed pepper, green beans, a roll, a carton of milk and a piece of fruit. It was not only the low cost of the meal that was noted, but also that even a school system with a sharp eye on economy could serve stuffed peppers in the middle of winter.

Bob went on to recall what it was like during a cold snowy winter in 1917 when he was working for E.A. Fuller in his store. Although that was eighty-three years ago, customers would still recognize the building, for it's the site of the former Belchertown Pharmacy. Bob made nine dollars a week. During the winter months they stocked a supply of potatoes, onions, turnip, squash and cabbage. Most of these were from local or nearby farms, and by this time of the year they were not very fancy. Some city markets handled hothouse cucumbers and tomatoes, and there may have been some rail shipments of other vegetables. But not in Belchertown. For fruit, there were oranges (in short supply), lemons and bananas (always by the bunch with a hang-up cord at the end). These were susceptible to freezing and were not always stocked in the coldest weather.

"Occasionally we splurged with grapes—malagas—that came in a small keg-like container, packed in ground cork. Reaching down into the cork and pulling the huge bunches from their hiding places was like a treasure hunt."

An advertisement for Fuller's grocery store, March 1910.

As you walk down the aisle of a market today and pile your carrier high with items that could not have been found north of Florida in 1917, remember how Bob felt when in 1959, he marveled at having the miracle of stuffed peppers in January.

Doris Dickinson

WINTER

P lease Cancel Recent Order for Six Coconut Palms!"
     The above title was the heading for an article that Bob Jackson wrote, almost fifty years ago, for his "Steeple" column. A "near record-breaking blizzard," in late February of 1958, had brought the same conditions we recently experienced in New England. Schools were closed, "even into Springfield." Bob taught in Springfield. It "gave us a chance to shovel in peace." He gave applause to the "Belchertown snow-movers" who had "been fully ready for the gale and their efforts brought local roads into condition quickly and efficiently," much like today. What was most enjoyable about this piece, to me, is that Bob harkens back to his boyhood days. I thought maybe others would find the same enjoyment and appreciate the changes that have come about.

> *When we are hit by a blizzard, we think back to our boyhood, when no roads were cleared, and sleds or sleighs were the order of the day. Now, our efforts are all in the direction of keeping autos off the highways until the clearing is done and back onto the highways in order that our economy may keep going.*
>
> *Along about this time of the year the boys were sliding down Maple Street and Jabish Street. With conditions right on "Depot Hill," you could go right up over the railroad bridge on your own power and coast down to the flat near Stacy's [near where Checkers is located today]. Or on "Creamery Hill" [Jabish Street] you could go all the way across the bridge over Jabish Brook and part way up the rise toward the present Route 9. On Jabish Street our worry was that we might meet up with a sled-load of ice, toiling up the hill from Dyer's Pond. How many of you have ever been on a double-ripper? Does any kid get his money's worth from a sled today? But we had no skis.*
>
> *For that matter, have you ever seen a horse ball? That was a big hunk of ice knocked off a horse's foot where it had accumulated until the animal was actually traveling on rounded stilts three or four inches high. They were scattered all over the roads. These balls of ice could be deadly weapons when hurled in anger by little boys walking home from school. About this time of the year, Belchertown High had its Annual Sleigh Ride. With Tom Allen safely perched on the front seat with the driver,*

Winter

A winter scene on South Main Street.

we huddled under blankets and were thrilled by the presence of warm cuddleness only five or six layers of woolen skirts and underwear away. Our destination was usually a hotel in Palmer or Amherst, where we had dinner and then returned slowly, accompanied by the music of genuine sleigh bells and the melodies of the period.

It is close to zero as I write this and an icy wind is abroad. Forty years ago, I would be huddled close to the "kitchen fire" or the "sittin' room fire" and dreading two things: going to the bathroom and then going to bed. If you have never "gone out back" on a winter evening—if you have never climbed into a bed in a room that has felt no heat but yours since last October—you just can't appreciate modern living, brother.

It was below zero this morning when I ventured out to get my daily paper. The weatherman said the wind chill factor was twenty-five degrees below zero. But the sun is shining now, the icicles are dripping and the roads are clear. I am nice and warm in our little home and reading old *Sentinels*. Thanks, Bob.

Bob always closed his column with a bit of poetry. I think I will follow suit today with a section from "Cold" by Amherst poet Robert Francis.

> Under the glaring and sardonic sun,
> Behind the icicles and double glass,
> I huddle, hoard, hold out, hold on, hold on.

Doris Dickinson

Visit us at
www.historypress.net